CHEN SHI MIN

Selected and Current Works

THE MASTER ARCHITECT SERIES III

CHEN SHI MIN

Selected and Current Works

First published in Australia in 1998 by
The Images Publishing Group Pty Ltd
ACN 059 734 431
6 Bastow Place, Mulgrave, Victoria, 3170
Telephone (61 3) 9561 5544 Facsimile (61 3) 9561 4860

National Library of Australia Cataloguing-in-Publication Data

      Chen, Shi Min, 1935–.
      Chen Shi Min: selected and current works.

      Bibliography.
      Includes index.
      ISBN 1 875498 89 3.

      1. Chen, Shi Min, 1935–. 2. Architecture, Chinese.
      3. Architecture, Modern—20th century—China. I. Title.
      (Series: Master architect series. III).

  720.951

Edited by Stephen Dobney
Designed by The Graphic Image Studio Pty Ltd,
Mulgrave, Australia
Film by Scanagraphix Australia Pty Ltd
Printed in Hong Kong

Contents

INTRODUCTION

Foreword

The Versatile Architecture of Chen Shi Min
By Michael J. Crosbie

The architecture of Chen Shi Min can be read as a record in microcosm of Chinese architecture over the past 40 years—in particular the blossoming of architecture in China in the past two decades. Within his oeuvre is found architecture scaled to the state, and architecture that responds to the more intimate scale of the community. Here are buildings that are products of Chen Shi Min's early experience within a large, government-run architectural institute. More recent projects reflect the opening of China to the West over the past decade, during which time Chen Shi Min has become head of his own private architectural firm. While most of the projects here are of recent vintage, together they capture the various phases of Chen Shi Min's career.

And a varied career it has been. Born in Sichuan Province in 1935, Chen Shi Min studied at the Chongqing Institute of Architecture and Engineering. For a dozen years he worked at the Beijing Institute of Industrial Architecture and Design (BIIAD) before he and his family were sent to work in a remote part of the countryside during the Cultural Revolution. Throughout the 1970s Chen Shi Min continued to practice with BIIAD, working on nationally important projects. With the advent of China's "Open Door" policy in the 1980s, Chen Shi Min grasped the opportunity to establish an architectural practice in Hong Kong. This experience brought him into contact with architecture firms around the world, from which he was able to draw on elements of contemporary Western practice. Through his work, Chen Shi Min endeavors to promote a new architectural language drawn from Chinese vernacular culture, its history, arts, traditional design philosophies, and methodologies, and express it through modern construction technology. It is Chen Shi Min's view that this is the only way to create a unique identity for contemporary Chinese architecture. The most striking features of the work in this book are the truly national-scale projects, the towers of striking geometric complexity, and the buildings that seem to capture the vernacular qualities of traditional Chinese architecture. Within these three arenas, Chen Shi Min exemplifies the important Chinese architecture of his time.

Chen Shi Min is not only one of the most influential architects in China, but also one of the first to introduce Chinese architecture to other parts of the world. In 1994, in recognition of his accomplishments, he was awarded the title "Design Master," an honor given to less than a dozen other architects in China.

A State Scale

Architecture scaled to the state is distinguished by the grandness of its gesture. Chen Shi Min's work abounds with buildings that reflect the scale of the state—large projects that accommodate the great throngs of one of the world's most populous countries. Some of these projects encompass entire city precincts, such as the design for Shenzhen's new downtown (page 18). Here, the scale is indeed super, encompassing almost 4 million square meters. The symmetrical plan stretches along an axial arrangement and is distinguished by towers amid sweeping green spaces, and the separation of pedestrian and vehicular traffic. Chen Shi Min based the design on ancient Chinese city planning principles; however, the planning ideas of Le Corbusier's Radiant City are also abundantly evident.

Another project of great civic scale, which also borrows from Le Corbusier, is Chen Shi Min's design for a residential development in Shenzhen, in southern China (page 234). The scheme, which won an international design competition, breaks down the large scale of the 400,000-square-meter development by dividing the residences into five neighborhoods, each defined by a complex of faceted high-rises. Chen Shi Min articulates the surfaces of these buildings and sites them so that they work within the Shenzhen climate, maximizing natural light and ventilation. What really mediates this super-scale development with the needs of individual residents is the separation of vehicular traffic (accommodated in a series of tunnels that run under the site) from pedestrian traffic (which meanders freely though the site). The pedestrian paths link to stores, schools, day care, and other amenities.

The architect's scheme for Fengrun Garden (page 230), also in Shenzhen, is of a comparable size. But here, instead of high-rise towers and vast open spaces, Chen Shi Min distributes low-scale buildings throughout the site, with smaller, more intimate gardens between them. There is a scattering of high-rise buildings at the periphery, and meandering paths connect the various residential blocks.

A large-scale project with a more Western flavor, now under construction, is the Rose Garden development in Shenzhen (page 220). The centrepiece of this composition is a 30-story apartment block around which are arrange lower-rise 12-story buildings that form a wall about the site. The facades have a distinctly European appearance, yet the central building also suggests the super-scale towers of the high Socialist Realism period that one finds in many Chinese and Russian cities. The scale is softened with colorful materials that respond to the garden setting.

Chen Shi Min's exposure to Western architectural ideas is abundantly evident in his super-scaled design for the International Conference and Exhibition Center in Qingdao, China (page 58). The most striking element of the design is the long, open greensward composed of five plazas that stretches along a north–south axis, and onto which the center fronts. The building itself is expressive in its light, wave-like forms, which intimate the lofty heights promised by new technology.

Towers of Delight

If the architectural expression of Western capitalism is found in the skyscraper, then Chen Shi Min has discovered a way to meld East and West, redefining this building type for Asian contexts. His tower designs exhibit much creative energy and delight in this most versatile building form.

The China Construction Corporation Complex tower in Chongqing, China (page 208), is at once a bold, contemporary design and a sensitive response to the hot climate and local building traditions. To a Western eye the compartmental nature of the tower suggests plug-in electronic modules. But to local sensibilities the form reflects the tradition of building houses on stilts. The articulation of the tower's four elements allows the introduction of green space between them—shaded hanging gardens that are a welcome respite in Chongqing's hot climate. Chen Shi Min uses a similar approach in the design of another Chongqing tower—the Daxin Building (page 158)—which is part of an addition to an existing project. Roof gardens and shaded outdoor space in the sky provide relief in this crowded, humid city.

The design for the 68-story Huafu Center for a downtown site in Fuzhou, China (page 116), is striking in its use of tubular steel armature. Ever mindful of the climate, Chen Shi Min again incorporates open rooftop gardens in the design, while glass elevators afford sweeping views of the city. Another 68-story tower, this one in Jinan, China (page 130), takes traditional Chinese pagoda designs as its inspiration in arranging the hierarchy of office, apartment, and hotel spaces. At its summit is a needle-like spire that pierces the sky and dramatizes the tower's stature.

Chen Shi Min draws upon more traditional, Western architectural imagery in his design for the Shanglong Building in Shenzhen (page 88). Because the site is at the heart of an older neighborhood of the city, the traditional forms lend the tower an established, classical appearance. Inspired by more contemporary skyscraper design, Chen Shi Min's scheme for the Huanqing Building (page 202), also in Shenzhen, suggests the American influence of such masters of the tower as Raymond Hood and Hugh Ferris, in its strong vertical expression and setbacks, rising to a glistening climax at the tower's core.

A trio of towers for the skyline of Dalian, China (page 136), also reflect the influence of contemporary Western design on Chen Shi Min, who gave each of the buildings a distinctive crown. Because of the city's cold climate, the architect used concrete and stone cladding with smaller windows to minimize the tower's exposure to the elements.

Vernacular Overtures

Perhaps the most satisfying of Chen Shi Min's work are projects that grow out of the traditional architecture of China, reinterpreting the local vernacular in contemporary buildings. The Shatian Baofu Cemetery in Hong Kong (page 48) appears as a Chinese landscape painting, revealing its tripartite organization as one ascends the site. One enters through a gate and passes fountains and gardens which invite one to leave the earthly world behind. The centerpiece of the project is a five-story pagoda which serves as a transition to the third part, a row of Tang dynasty style houses that stretch along the side of a hill. These structures to honor the memory of departed ancestors are planned according to *feng shui*, the ancient Chinese principles of design.

Chen Shi Min combines Chinese vernacular architecture and influences from the West in his design for the Qilin Resort in Shenzhen (page 94), which takes the form of a series of villas sited in the hills. While the exteriors exude a sophisticated interpretation of traditional architecture, the interiors reflect a European sensibility. Designing in an urban context, the architect uses vernacular form judiciously in the Hotel Sinomonde (page 72), located in the Chinatown precinct of Montreal, Canada. The modernist hotel building is topped with Chinese tile roofs and calligraphic characters. Here the vernacular style is used to forge a cultural tie between the two countries.

Chen Shi Min culminates his vernacular design approach in a truly magnificent project: the Chinese Cultural Village in Nara, Japan (page 34). Here the architect exhibits great sensitivity to the two cultures—Japanese and Chinese—and celebrates the age-old links between them. The center of this project is a building based on a piece of 14th century Tang dynasty architecture, around which an entire tourist precinct is oriented. The broad, sweeping vistas from this building out over the low-rise housing, restaurants, shops, and recreational areas recall Chen Shi Min's handling of open space in many of his projects.

Such projects once again remind us that the architecture of Chen Shi Min grows from a fertile imagination, steeped in the traditions of both the East and the West.

Dr. Crosbie is an architect, critic, and professor, who writes about architecture and design from his home in Essex, Connecticut, USA.

Introduction

By Chen Shi Min

Architecture, as an artistic form of engineering, creates a culture that must interact closely with the social context of the times, with vernacular culture, with art and history, with lifestyles, and with geography and landscape. This architectural culture is constantly changing in response to social, economic, and technological developments.

A building without such a culture would lose the characteristics of the nature of architecture. Therefore, considerable effort should be put into exploring the legacy of our traditional culture and history in order to create architecture that is able to transform our lives and environments in a contemporary context.

Architecture and Environment

Architecture and environment are interrelated. A good design should be the result of a sensitive study of its environment; conversely, the architecture should be able to transform and enhance (add value to) its environment.

As architects, our mission is to create pleasant and functional spaces and environments. Inspiration and ideas for architectural design can often emerge from a thorough understanding of the project environment. However, it is not sufficient to create a building which simply fits into or matches its surroundings. I believe that good architecture should be created by its environment and that the environment should be transformed and enhanced by the architecture.

Nanhai Hotel (1986) is an example of how a design theme can be derived from its unique environment, and how the architecture, in return, can enrich and add a unique feature to its surroundings. Shenzhen Financial Center (1983), on the other hand, was an experiment in creating architecture that transformed its environment by emphasizing the relationship between the building and its urban context as an organic whole for the new city landscape. The design of the Gintian project (1991) was the result of developing key points as a principle to drive the design scheme. After thoroughly studying the site location, a unique design was developed which brings the external environment inside the building by means of a two-story glass-enclosed lobby. This illustrates again that architecture should be directly or indirectly the result of a sensitive observation of its natural environment and should, as far as possible, incorporate the beauty of nature into the artificial space. In return, the architecture adds to its surrounding.

Architectural Space

Architecture can be regarded as spatial planning and spatial relationships. Purposely created architectural space can bring to a building an "infectious power" and a sense of "vitality" that can last for centuries.

People understand architecture through the internal and external space created by a building. In a design sense, architecture can be regarded as spatial planning and spatial relationships. Architectural space is a sequence of spatial compositions according to a particular design order. For example, the architectural space of a hotel can be regarded as the sequence of entering the atrium space, proceeding to the lift lobby, and finally reaching the guest room, and so on. However, a building is not an isolated object: the internal space has an inseparable relationship with the surrounding external space. In other words, an architectural space is composed of both its internal and external spaces. The longevity of a piece of architecture, then, depends not only on the choice of building technologies, materials, and equipment, but also on the quality of its architectural space.

In order to attract the public eye, deliver its services, and maintain its economical value, a building should have "vitality." This requires a flexibility in the use of space which will allow the building to accommodate the changing demands imposed on architecture over time. In addition, a good architectural space can bring an "infectious power" into a building. For example, an old European church provides people with a sensation of spirituality; traditional Chinese imperial architecture, on the other hand, creates a grand and majestic impression. Both of them achieve different impressions through different architectural spaces.

In the light of these considerations, it has become one of my top priorities in design to pursue an architecture which embodies "infectious power," artistic appeal, and vitality. I believe that architectural space should be created according to functional requirements and environmental concerns. Architectural space can be identified by sequential changes or variations in scales, proportions, levels, and purposely selected building elements and materials. Sometimes, a technique of contrast is also used for this purpose. In the mini-gardens of Suzhou in China, this technique is successfully used to simulate a much bigger virtual space. The winning project of 160,000 square metres, Sig Plaza, in 1995 was the result of targeting architectural space as the driving design scheme for a modern high-rise building. In the design of Hotel Sinomonde in Montreal (1988), the atrium becomes a public space that is shared among the hotel, conference, and restaurant facilities. It provides an ideal internal space with an atmosphere that is warm, natural, and open in contrast to the harsh cold of a Montreal winter.

To design a modern building in China today, we not only have to address the needs of functionality and applicability, but also to take into account the flexibility, convertibility, and possible future expansion of the built space. In other words, to design a building with vitality, you need to include the flexibility for future use in your initial design. For example, the Tianan International Building (1988) uses a single spine structure to give tenants maximum flexibility in the use of space, allowing them to accommodate future changes due to market forces. Every time I design a building, I not only approach it from two-dimensional planning point of view, but also keep a three-dimensional perspective in mind to achieve the ultimate spatial outcome. Achieving distinctive architecture by combining "space," efficiency, and an attractive modern architectural language has become a key objective of my work.

Contemporary Architecture and Vernacular Culture

Different functional requirements, different project environments, and different regions and climates should result in different architectural forms. Although most modern buildings, particularly high-rises, are subject to the architectural trends of the time, they are also influenced by market demands and clients' individual tastes. I do not believe that a successful architecture can be the result of following a particular fashion or blindly implementing a particular design theory. In my years of practice, I never set on a particular style or followed one. The only way I develop the form of a building is to study the site, analyze the

circulation requirements, and determine the architectural space I would like to create. Based on the initial design concept, I choose an appropriate architectural language that will reflect the characteristics of the building's function and express its cultural and temporal context.

With the spread of internationalism, however, modern architecture is facing the risk of merging into one stereotype and gradually losing its individuality. To overcome this, we need to study the vernacular features of our culture and develop new styles that combine these characteristics with aspects of contemporary architecture and modern technologies. In the case of China, I believe there should be a balance between Chinese tradition and modern architecture. In each of my design projects I constantly seek to create such a unique identity.

One of my early attempts to find a unique architectural style was the Chinese Cultural Village in Nara, Japan (1986). Nara is the cultural center of Japan and its links with China span thousands of years. To highlight the cultural connection between the two nations, I purposely introduced into the project a classic piece of Tang Dynasty Chinese architecture—Hanyuan Palace. Moreover, the entire design was based on and extrapolated from the original Tang Dynasty style. From my point of view, this approach is the first level of "architectural integration:" a straightforward method of transposing traditional Chinese architectural design and styles into a foreign country.

The Hotel Sinomonde in Montreal (1988), on the other hand, used a different approach to combine traditional Chinese and modern Western architecture. This approach, which I call "form integration," involves bringing the classic elements and symbols of Chinese architecture, such as pavilions and gardens, into a very modern building. The main reason for such an approach in this case was the project's unique location in Montreal's Chinatown. This, then, is the second level of "integration" in architectural style.

The Architecture Cultural Center in Beijing (1995) represents the third level of architectural style integration, which I call "ideological integration." As the building will be used for the 20th

International Architectural Conference and the 21st Congress of UIA in Beijing in 1999—the end of 20th century—I thought it should reflect both traditional Chinese and modern architecture. To my mind, this is the most remarkable aspect of the entire design theme. As well as introducing traditional Chinese master plan concepts, I also applied the three most fundamental Chinese architectural elements—"door," "corridor," and "hall"—using ancient Chinese design methodologies. For example, the major spaces used by the conference hall, exhibition center, and lobby were located in the middle, according to the central axis concept of the Chinese "hall." Support services, such as lifts, circulation, and plant rooms, were symmetrically located at both sides of the central axis to form the "corridor." The main front entrance and the wide open space are a formalized interpretation of the Chinese "door;" an architectural metaphor of the saying that "everything should start from the door." This is a more sophisticated level of architectural integration of styles, as it brings Chinese ideological design concepts into a building with a 21st century architectural image. It involves "inspirational integration," which is more difficult than the other two levels described above. Therefore, to create a unique architectural design and identity, we need not only to have a thorough understanding of the building contents and function, but also, and most importantly, to choose the right architectural language and style to present them.

With the recent intensification of competition and the involvement of international architectural firms in China, the expectations of clients have changed dramatically. Many clients are deliberately seeking unconventional architectural products in terms of styles, forms, and functionality in order to "show off" their corporate "image". In these circumstances, to consistently produce distinguished architectural identity for the client has becomes our priority in design. The only way for Chinese architects to achieve this objective is by further exploring the legacy of our traditional Chinese culture and history, and integrating them into contemporary architecture. The recent China Construction Corporation Complex in Chongqing (1996) is one example of how to represent regional culture and geographical characteristics in their own architectural form.

Circulation and Transportation

As we know, the human circulation system plays a crucial role in allowing the life-energy to flow naturally throughout the body. A similar principle should be applied in architectural design, in terms of handling a building's internal circulation and external transportation, particularly in large, multi-function, multi-level complexes. In some cases, circulation and transportation can be used as the guiding principle in the organization of building spaces, layout plans, and even in the architectural form and style. A building's success is sometimes judged by the way in which these factors are handled. In the case of a comprehensive building complex which combines hotel, office, apartment, retail, and parking functions, I believe there is a need to design the circulation system as one would with an airport: it should be an efficient, integrated development.

The design for the Shenzhen Railway Station (1989), for example, was the result of seeking a new solution to the problem of high-volume circulation and intense use of space in a public building, drawing on my understanding of architectural modernism. Because the building was to be used as both a domestic and an international terminal, functions such as customs, immigration, a hotel, shops, restaurants, and other support services had to be accommodated in addition to the normal railway station functions. I applied the same design principles used in airports to handle the circulation demands for this project.

The Tianan International Building (1988) is another good example of solving traffic and circulation problems, in this case for a large, modern building complex containing a hotel, high-rise offices, apartments, and a multi-level shopping podium. An underground "transportation zone" allows vehicles to circulate and access the various components of the complex without interfering with the already over-congested street-level transportation system.

In the Hongji Commercial Center in Tianjin (1994), parking and traffic restrictions in the nearby streets prompted the creation of a "central traffic zone" under the proposed building to handle all the transportation and circulation. This concept, in fact, was instrumental in the proposal winning the international design competition. The three examples above demonstrate that efficient, well-structured and integrated circulation and transportation systems should be considered key elements in design and should be dealt with at all stages, from the master plan and functional layout of each floor, through to the space organization; they may even influence a building's structure and form. In addition, the efficiency of circulation is also an important factor contributing to the economic success of a development, particularly for large modern commercial complexes.

New Challenges

21st Century Architecture

Very soon the world will step in the 21st century. Finding ways to participate in the transitional changes and to design buildings which reflect the "information age"—within a Chinese context—will be one of the exciting objectives of Chen Shi Min Architects. In the Futian Residential Development urban planning project in Shenzhen (1997) I have explored some concepts for a 21st century Chinese living environment. Fresh air, natural light, adequate green space, convenient transportation, and community services are key elements in the creation of modern metropolitan suburbs that break away from the existing over-congested, over-developed, and over-polluted conurbations.

Urban Residential Design and Development

At the end of the 20th century, the population of China will exceed 1.4 billion people. Coping with the increasing demands for housing and providing an adequate modern living environment for such a large population, particularly in major metropolises such as Shanghai, Guangzhou, and Beijing, has become an impending issue for Chinese architects and planners. Further study is required on how to effectively develop and utilize our limited land and resources and revitalize old building sites and areas for future development.

Conclusion

In retrospect, over more than 40 years of practice I have come to the conclusion that architectural design is a serious activity requiring hard work. As architects, we have the enormous responsibility of delivering products that meet the needs of clients, the public, and society at large. Unfortunately, in today's China, as in all contemporary societies, a great pressure has been placed upon architects to create architecture as a "commodity." It has become an increasing challenge for all of us to find a balance between art and commerce. I believe that architecture is a public art and that it is our important role, as architects, to promote new architectural images, directions, and methodologies. We should be able to create architecture that transforms our lives and our environments, and that satisfies the increasing demands for functionality, economy, and style.

In the meantime, we need to maintain the balance in architectural expression in order that it reflects the urban context, the environment, and the geographic landscape. To achieve this, we need to avoid formalistic design approaches and monotonous and meaningless building blocks. Instead, we need to persistently review and redefine architectural methodologies and practices to be in line with a new generation of buildings and technologies, to capture the very nature of architecture, to understand the environment, to reflect the times and spaces in which we are living. In other words, to feel the pulse of today and the future. This is the mission for contemporary architects.

SELECTED & CURRENT WORKS

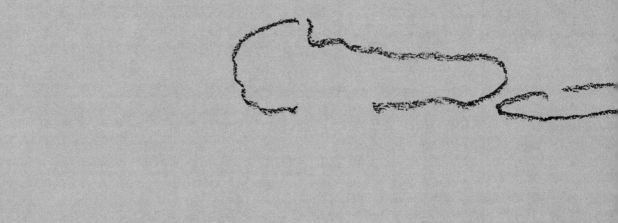
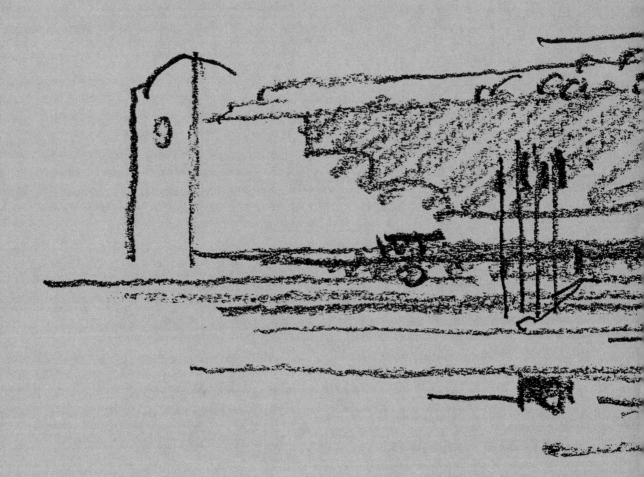

PUBLIC BUILDINGS

New Downtown Shenzhen

Design 1996
Shenzhen, China
Shenzhen Urban Planning & Land Administration Bureau
Site area: 4,138,600 square meters
Total floor area: 3,779,400 square meters
International competition runner-up

The architect was invited, together with consultants from the United States, Canada, France, and Singapore, to prepare a design for the new city center.

The design responds to two general conditions which affect all cities in China: a large population and a scarcity of land. Accordingly, the design aims to change the present overcrowded and polluted metropolitan center into a comfortable, modern space with green areas separated from vehicular traffic, with fresh air, and with beautiful architecture appropriate to the 21st century.

The design brief stipulated a plot ratio of 1:8 and a general height limit to 100 meters, with a few buildings limited to 200 meters. The plan departs from the existing method of dividing blocks, instead providing green space between blocks and comfortable green areas within each block. All these green spaces are connected to create a trans-block pedestrian passage system linked to the main buildings and commercial areas. In this way, a vertical separation of pedestrians and vehicles is achieved.

The city hall and the shady green space around it form the central element; along the axis, groups of lower buildings form a series of squares. This brings the scenery of the Lianhuashan area into the city, to the benefit of all city residents.

1

1 Aerial view of center square from north
2 Master plan

18

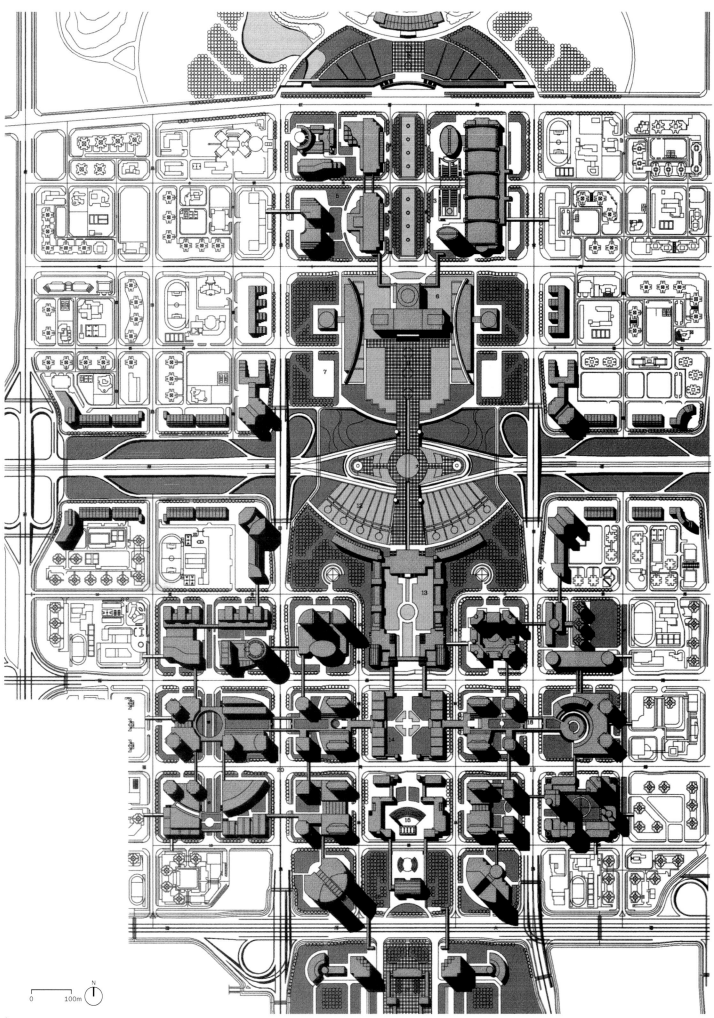

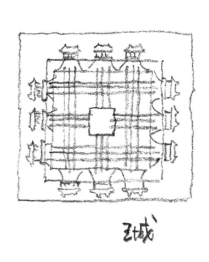

元城

中国传统城市
规划格局

3

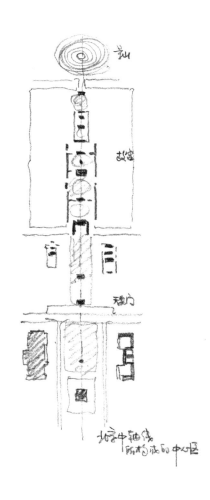

北京中轴线
所构成的中心区

4

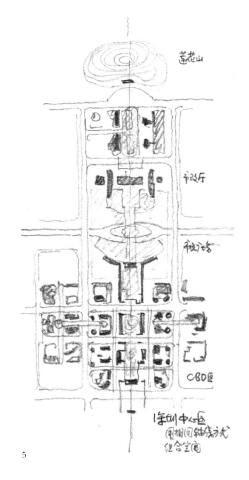

深圳中心区
用相同轴线方式
组合空间

5

3   Ancient Chinese city planning
4   Central axis in Beijing, China
5   New city planning in Shenzhen
6&7 Perspective sketches showing central shopping area and transportation
8   General view of model from south

6

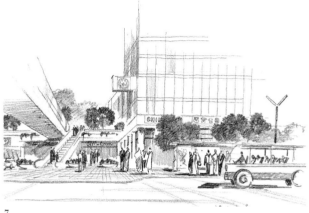

7

8

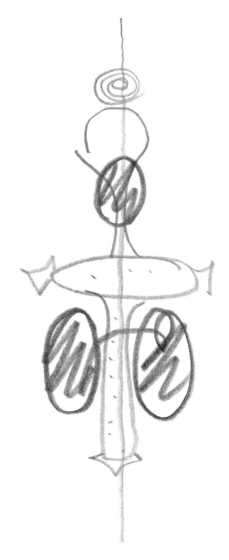

9

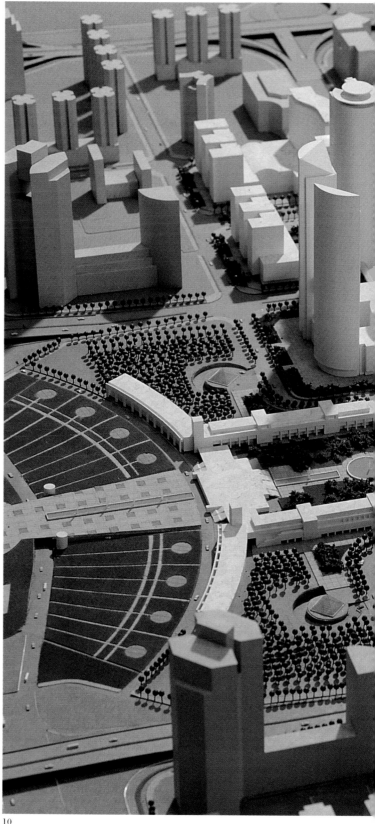

10

9 Sketch of city planning structure
10 Aerial view of central business district, new downtown
11 Bird's-eye view of model

11

Shenzhen City Hall

Design 1996
Shenzhen, China
Shenzhen Construction Bureau
Site area: 161,200 square meters
Total floor area: 120,000 square meters
Reinforced concrete
Stone, curtain wall, colored metal panel

This project is located at the center of Shenzhen's new downtown. It acts as the connection point between the Lianhua Hill scenic area and the City Hall Plaza. In order to emphasize this connection, a cavity 60 meters long and 25 meters high is inserted in the building. This ensures the Lianhua Hill scenery can be seen from the City Hall Plaza through the open cut cavity.

The new City Hall consists of government offices, an assembly hall, and other function rooms. Based upon the central axis space planning principle, the city museum is placed on the left, and the art gallery and concert hall are placed on the right. The wide central staircases and the symmetrical planning draw on historical Chinese design precedents.

The simple cubic form and the unique structure of the City Hall building symbolize the open nature of the municipal government, and are in contrast with conventional Chinese city hall design.

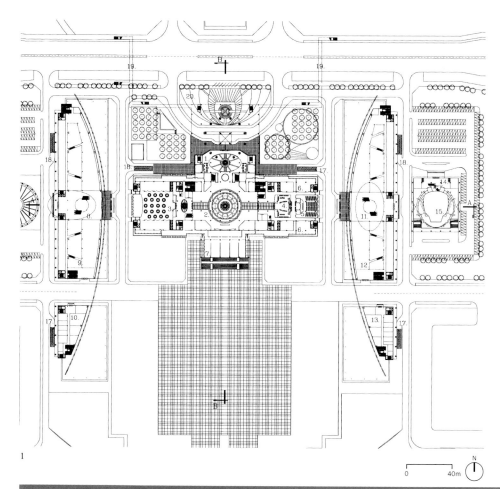

1

2

3

1   Master plan
2   View from the square
3   Concept sketch
4   Aerial view from north

4

Shenzhen Railway Station

Design/Completion 1989/1992
Shenzhen, China
Construction Administration of Shenzhen Municipal People's
Government and Shenzhen Railway Station
Site area: 28,600 square meters
Total floor area: 93,790 square meters
Reinforced concrete
Tile, curtain wall
Joint venture with Shenzhen Project & Research Institute of NMIC

This project involves a renovation of the
Shenzhen Railway Station complex, which
contains offices, 300 hotel rooms,
department stores, restaurants, and
recreation facilities in addition to the
station itself. It is also intended to provide
facilities for customs and immigration
between the cities of China and Hong
Kong.

The main public transport interchange is
at the front of the station. Because of the
limited size of the site, the entrances are
placed at the east and west sides along the
railway lines, and the waiting area is built
over the lines. The general traffic
circulation pattern is up to enter and
down to exit. Arriving passengers go
directly to the east square; around this

Continued

1

2

1 Perspective sketch
2 General view from east
3 Street view from north
4 View of elevation from northeast
5 General view from east across square

3

4

5

square, an overpass brings vehicles into the station, so that a vertical separation of pedestrians and vehicles is achieved.

The location of the project determined the architectural space of the building. A multi-layered, multi-dimensional structure was required to ensure easy access from all directions. The dimensions of the main building—215 meters wide and only 30 meters deep—dictated a plan composed of linear "belts." Four vertical traffic systems were designed, permitting functions within the complex to be grouped or utilized separately. In this way, a clear passenger flow and simplified passenger management is achieved. This linear plan is more like that of an airport, and represents a departure from the traditionally centralized model of Chinese railway stations.

In order to satisfy the client's request for a building of no less than 50 meters in height, and to avoid the possible sense of oppression this height might bring to the square in front of the station, the tower is designed in a curve which becomes slender towards the top. On the four corners, four quartered spheres are used to increase the sense of stability of the whole building.

The project has a visual simplicity and sense of movement that are strongly linked to its function. The hotel room balconies on the tower stretch out to reduce the contrast with the podium, and to communicate the volume of the tower. The facade of the podium is a combination of solid walls and glass curtain walls, which bring to mind clouds floating in the sky. The circular windows emphasize the flow of traffic within the building and are also a reminder of the traditional round gates at many Chinese railway stations. In this context, the circle suggests that Shenzhen is the southern gate of the mainland.

Two materials are used on the facade: ceramic tiles and glass. Stainless steel panels are inlaid on the corners, combining simplicity with a sense of industrialization. At the main entrance, red steel frames and a red gate add color to the building.

6   Station signage
7   Entrance gate
Opposite:
      Pedestrian access

6

7

9 Sketch plan of ground level
10 Sketch plan of passenger waiting hall
11 Study elevation
12 Entrance gate from inside of entrance hall

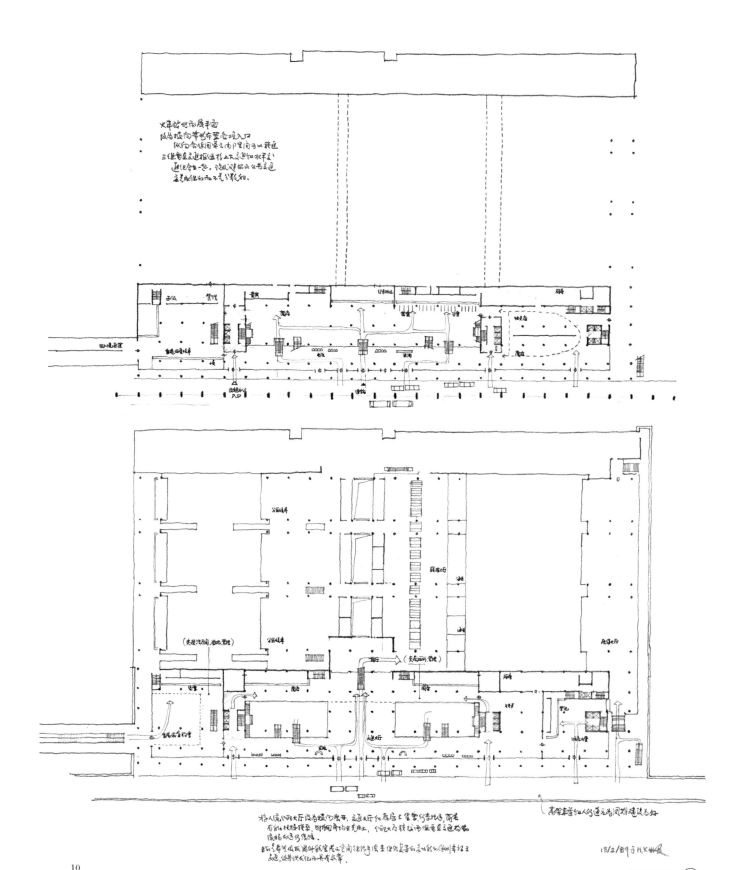

10

30

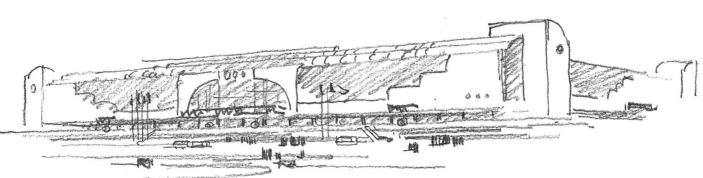

2/4/89 几经体味，未来现情钟楼
柔如向情，造型质疑
了m 60 全为基础了。

世良 太古

11

12

13   Perspective sketch of entrance hall
14   Entrance hall interior from north
15   Perspective sketch of passenger waiting hall
16   Passenger waiting hall

13

14

15

16

Chinese Cultural Village

Design 1986
Nara, Japan
Nara China Culture Village Co. Ltd
Site area: 4,000,000 square meters
Total floor area of main building: 30,000 square meters
Concrete, steel
Glass tile, brick, paint, wood
In cooperation with Seed Consultants Co. Ltd, Nara (Japan)

Nara is an ancient cultural city and also a world-famous tourist destination in Japan. The city was based on the ancient Chinese capital of Changan, and some pieces of Tang dynasty architecture still remain today.

The Chinese Cultural Village project reinforces the historical link between the two nations and promotes cultural exchange. The design of the village is rich in the representation of Chinese culture, and the buildings and the overall plan embody Chinese architectural tradition.

The main structure of the village is a copy of Hanyuandian, a 1360-year-old piece of Tang dynasty architecture. This building is magnificent, with flying eaves, pavilions, staircases, and covered corridors. It serves as the focus of the whole project, which develops with the topography and applies the traditional axis and use of space. There is a clear distinction between layers, and a dramatic contrast is created which starts from the gate and proceeds to the main structure, where the whole project reaches a climax.

Some 1,800,000 tourists are expected to visit the village annually—up to 10,000 per day in the busy season. The major functions of the village—commercial center, restaurant area, front gate, minority nationality areas, recreation center, and children's playground—form separate precincts, each with its own distinctive architectural character. Easy access is ensured between these precincts for service vehicles and site management. Grouping the functions in this way also allows the construction to be phased.

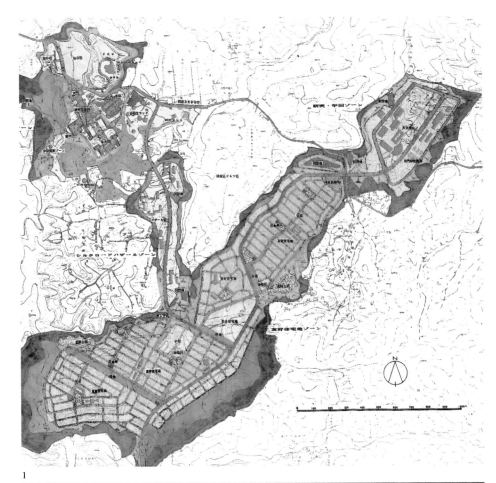

1

2

34

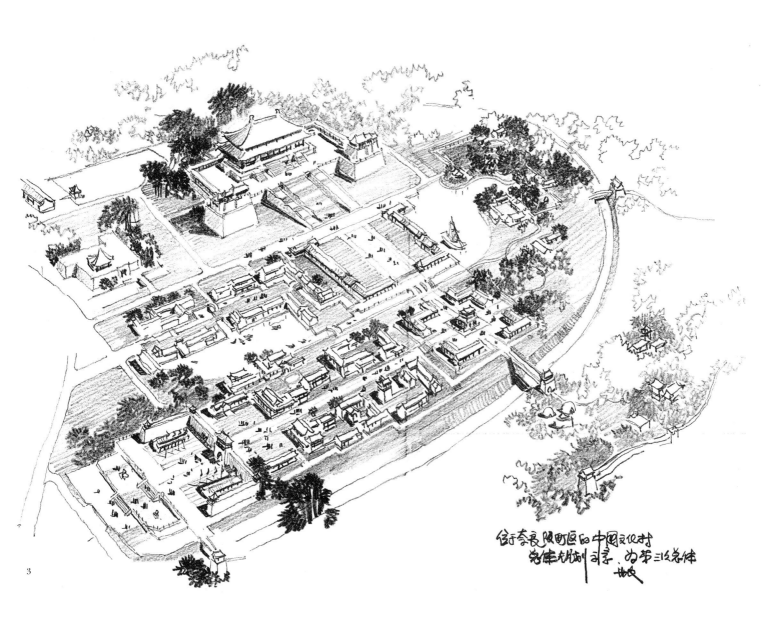

3

徐李畏原町区的中国文化村
总体规划方案 为第三次总体
地区

1 Master plan, including Chinese Cultural Village and new housing development
2 Aerial view of the whole village
3 Study sketch: overall view

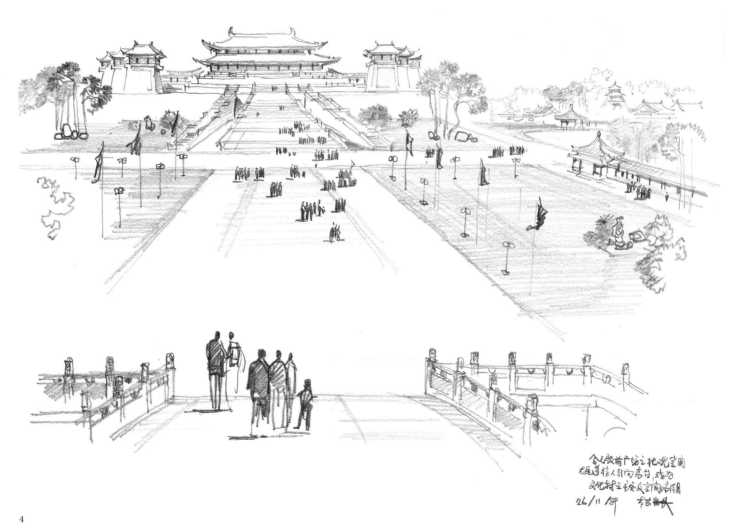

含元殿前广场之北观宝阁
左展廊指人引向意台，成为
文化节之舞及主阁阁剧阶
26/11/89 李志樵民

西市，为人流之集散
细部动春坊世之名共传统了坊
29/11/89 樵民

4   Study sketch of view from central axis
5   Sketch of shopping square
6&7 The reproduction of Hanyuandian, an ancient building in Xian, China
8   Concept sketch of Chinese garden

6

7

8

Foreign Trade Center

Competition 1992
Shenzhen, China
China Shenzhen Foreign Trade Center Ltd
Site area: 105,981 square meters
Total floor area: 400,000 square meters
Reinforced concrete
Stone, curtain wall
In cooperation with Peddle Thorp Architects (Australia)

This project involves the renovation and expansion of an old storage building. The new development comprises a group of buildings with large exhibition spaces, a conference hall, an office tower, and a five-star hotel. It also contains apartment, finance, information, shopping, and recreation facilities.

The project is divided into four building groups according to the functions of hotel, conference, office, and exhibition. Each component has its own independent activity space, circulation, and access to the outdoor open space. The buildings are connected by a well-designed circulation system. Additional open space is located along the river bank to afford wide open views.

The buildings have a variety of curved forms, giving the development a unified architectural identity.

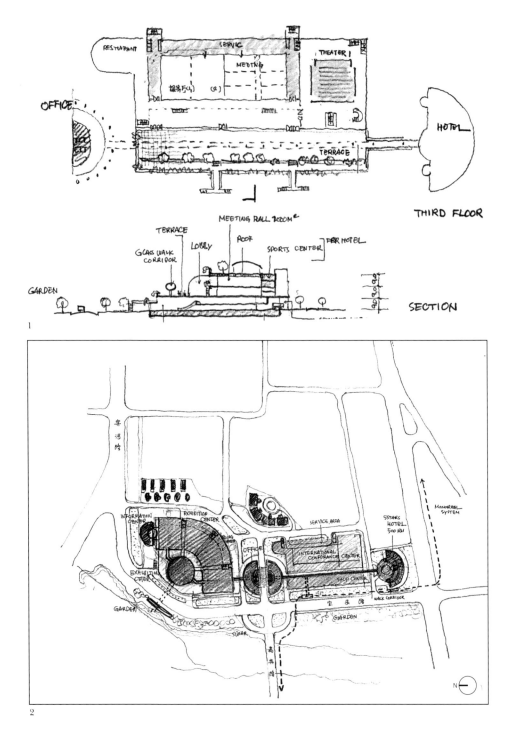

1

2

38

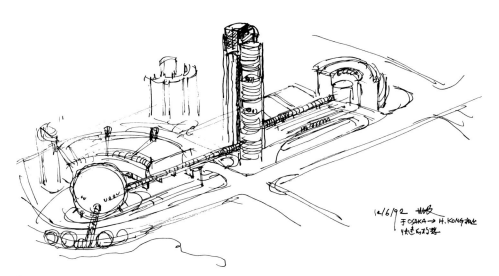

3

1 Conference hall plan
2 Site master plan
3 Concept sketch
4 Aerial view from southeast

4

Architecture Cultural Center, Beijing

Design/Completion 1995/1999
Beijing, China
Ministry of Construction, The State Administration Building Materials
Industry, China State Construction Engineering Corporation
Site area: 15,000 square meters
Total floor area: 63,000 square meters
Reinforced concrete, steel
Stone, curtain wall, metal panel
Winning international competition entry

This project is designed for the 20th International Architectural Conference and 21st Congress of the Union of International Architects, to be held in Beijing in 1999. It includes a conference hall, exhibition space, lecture halls, and a large number of offices. The objective of the design is to create a contemporary architecture that is able to blend Chinese culture, history, and architecture with modern technology for the next century.

The east side of the site borders the main street of Beijing. Considering the height limitation of 60 meters and the requirement of maintaining the two existing buildings, a T-shaped plan is adopted. On the center axis is the conference hall and exhibition space, while the two office towers are on the wings. The two building towers, centered on the main entrance, are placed facing the main road in order to create a distinctive architectural image. Wide staircases lead to a broad terrace which compensates for the limited space in the front square. The entire architectural space forms distinct layers, allowing easy access and flexibility in use.

Gate, hall, and corridor are the three essential elements in the Chinese master plan. Here, the major spaces of conference hall, exhibition space, and atrium are placed on the central axis, equating to the traditional concept of "hall." Other supporting services, such as the lifts, stairs, lavatories, and service rooms are symmetrically placed at either side of the central axis to form the "corridor." The main front entrance and wide open space together formalize the grand "gate."

According to ancient Chinese architectural methodology, a building starts from the "gate tower" and gradually extends to other building entities. Thus, the elevation design of the building is derived from the "gate tower" concept. The grand terrace, central axis space planning, and elegantly curving roof—elements of the traditional Chinese architectural language—are applied here to create a unique contemporary building. This is an "inspiration/integration" of Chinese tradition and modern architecture.

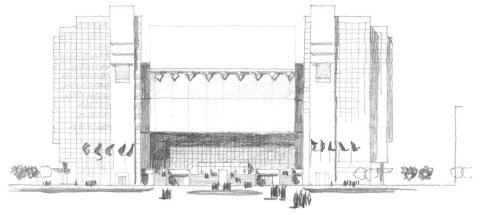

1

2

40

1 Elevation sketch
2 General view of model from southeast
3 Aerial view of model showing the conference hall and exhibition space
  on the center axis and office towers on the wings

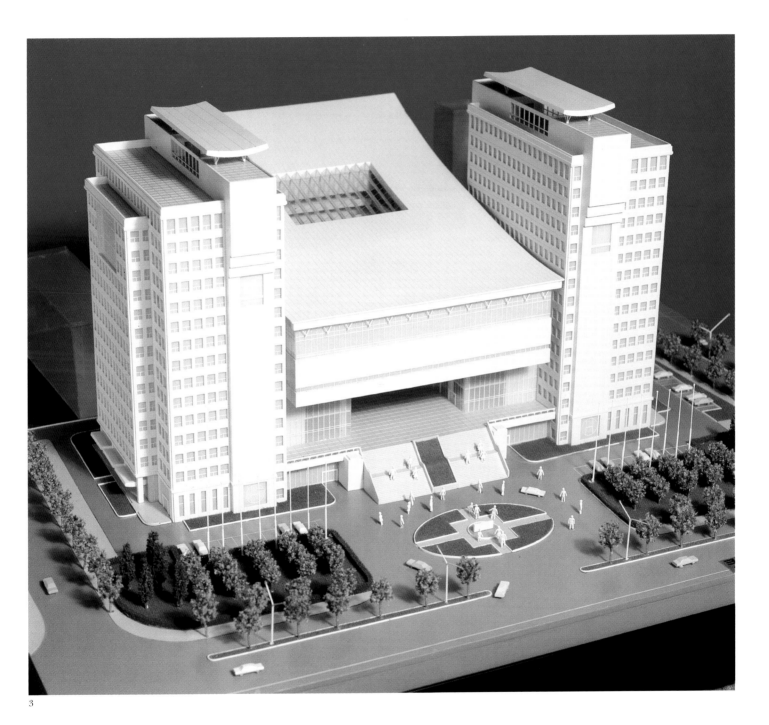

3

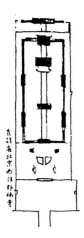

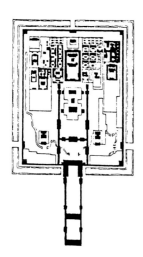

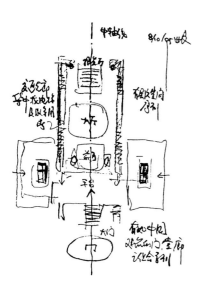

5

6

5 Sketch plan: gate, hall, and corridor are the three elements in traditional
  Chinese design
6 General view from the square (east)

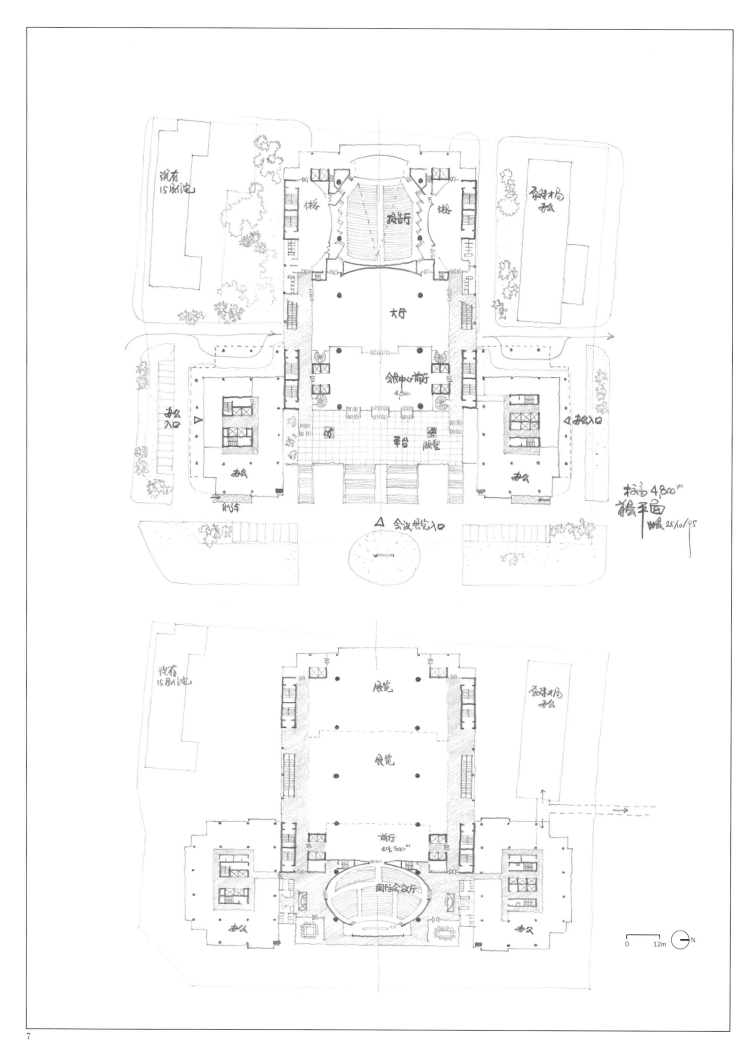

7   First floor plan (above); third floor plan (below)
8   Sketches showing the development wof the traditional Chinese concept of "gate tower"
9   Section sketch
10 Study sketch of elevation

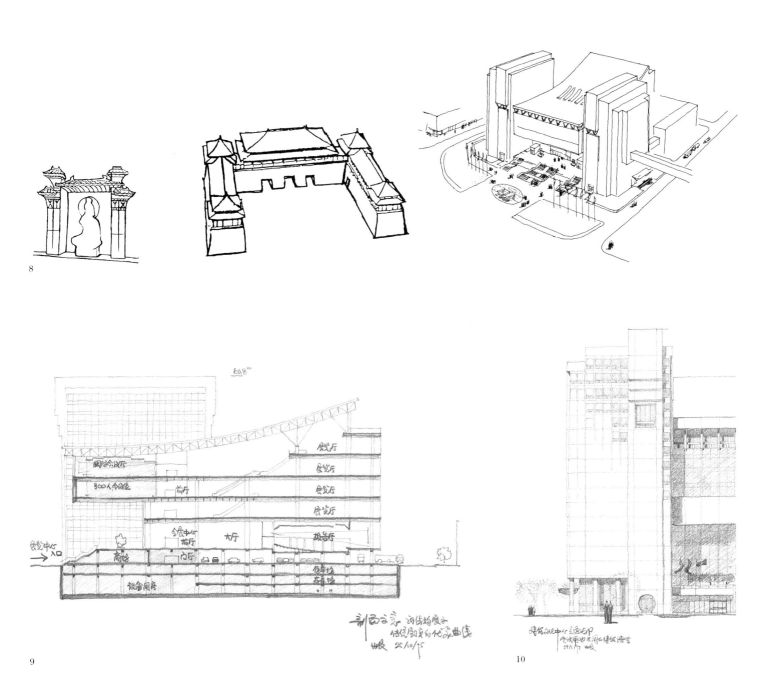

8

9

10

The Flying Saucer Nightclub

Design/Completion 1988/1991
Shenzhen, China
Shenzhen UFO Nightclub Co. Ltd
1,500 square meters
Steel structure
Glass, metal panel, wood
Winning competition entry

This nightclub is on the top level of the sixth floor podium of the International Trading Center building in Shenzhen. The umbrella-shaped external rooftop structure of the podium and the custom-designed interiors create a unique "flying saucer-like" architectural space.

The circular internal space comprises two floors. The lower level serves as the central hall, containing a circular dance floor, a dining space, and peripheral observing areas and bars. The upper level is formed by a group of "airplane-like" cabins. Each cabin has its own karaoke compartment. Through the cabin windows, patrons can view the evening performance on the lower level.

The materials, lighting, color selection, and other interior details are designed to create an atmosphere of mystery, speed, and tranquillity, evoking a sense of outer space.

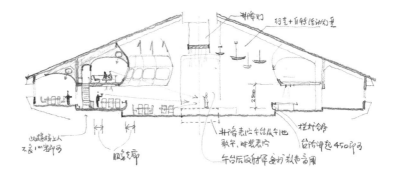

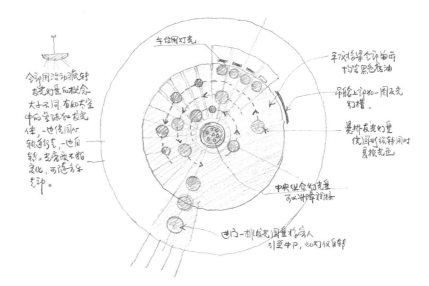

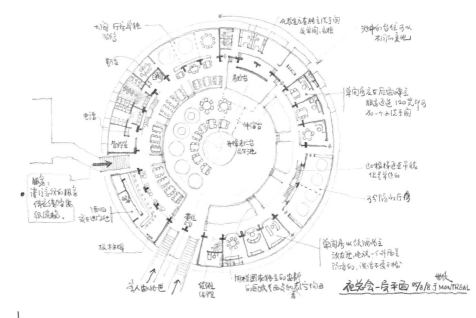

1 Sketches of section (above), lower level plan (middle), and upper level plan (below)
2 Sketch of the main hall
3 View of seating area in hall
4 Overall view of hall
5 View of restaurant
6 View of entrance
7 View of bar

2

3

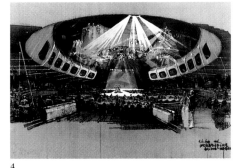

4

5

6

7

Shatian Baofu Cemetery

Design/Completion 1986/1989
Hong Kong, China
China Overseas Building Development Co. Ltd
Site area: 24,000 square meters
Open area: 22,000 square meters
Concrete
Roof tile, glass, paint
Joint venture with Chung Hua Nan Architects Ltd Hong Kong

The project is ideally located, with hills to the back and ocean scenery. It is enclosed on three sides by hills, and the only opening overlooks the city. The master plan limits use to a cemetery and a memorial to ancestors.

To blend the project with the natural scenery and environment, and to enrich it with Chinese culture and elegance, the architects divided the project into three parts. The prologue is a passage formed by the gate, staircases, sculpture, fountains, pools, and an attractive park. The second part begins with a five-story pagoda housing a statue of the Buddha. Around this is clustered a group of houses. This second part serves as the core of the space and a point of transition along the axis. The third part makes use of the steep topography to include three rows of one- and two-story houses with simple Tang dynasty appearance. Each row has its own passages and a view of the sea and the city. According to principles of *feng shui*, it is an ideal site. The three parts combine to form a tranquil, intimate, fresh, and beautiful temple-like architecture, inspiring visitors' memory of and respect for their ancestors.

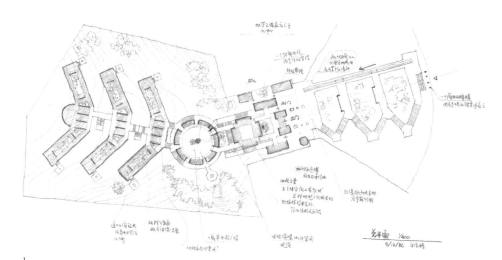

1

2

1 Site plan
2 View from south
3 Concept sketch

3

3/9 /89　为宝福山作绿松想
为那些玩获取观争利艺
地良

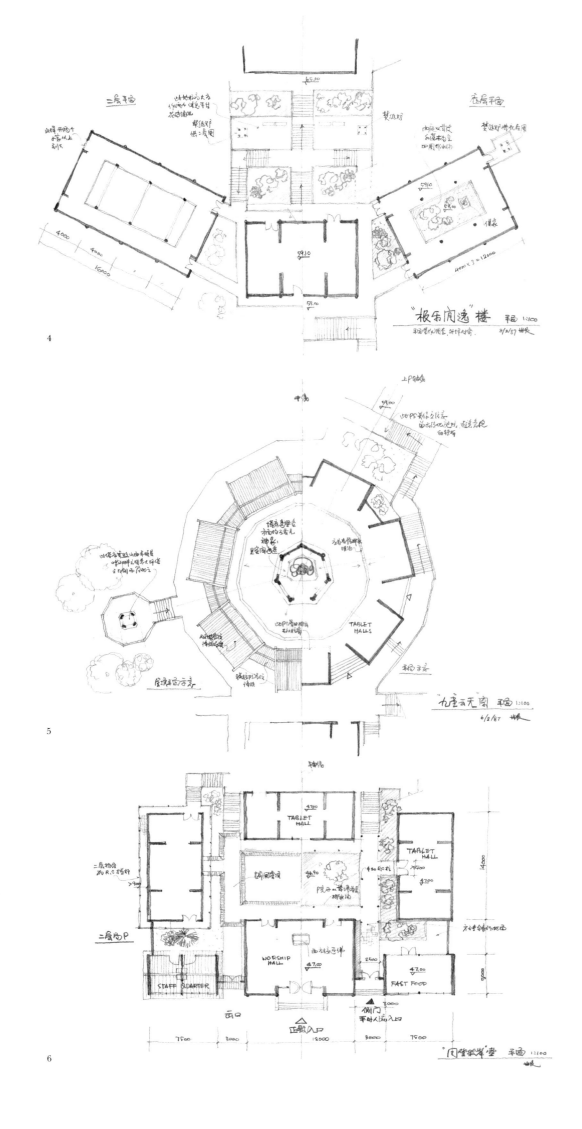

4

5

6

"极乐闲逸"楼 平面 1:100

"九座云天窗"平面 1:100

6/2/87

"闲座放荼楼" 平面 1:100

TABLET HALLS

TABLET HALL

TABLET HALL

WORSHIP HALL

STAFF QUARTER

FAST FOOD

二层房P

正殿入口

侧门

50

7

8

9

10

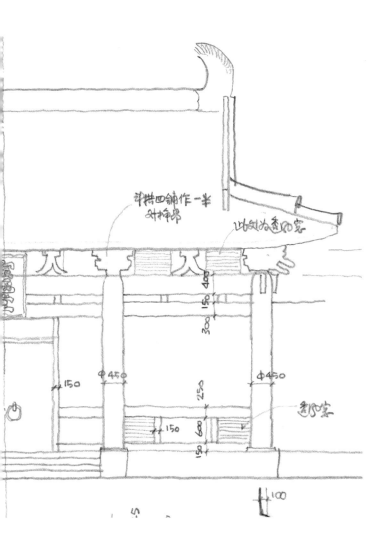

斗栱四铺作一半
对称部

此刻为香炉室

Φ450   Φ450

郭宗

11

12

13

9　Elevation sketch of worship hall
10　View of tablet hall from north
11　Individual tablet house
12　Roof detail
13　View of central courtyard

Shopping Mall in New Downtown

Design 1997
Shenzhen, China
Shenzhen Urban Planning & Land Administration Bureau
Site area: 58,207 square meters
Total floor area: 58,434 square meters
Concrete structure
Roof tile, glass, tile, metal panel
Joint venture with Peddle Thorp Architects (Australia)
Winning international competition entry

Adjacent to the two shopping parks in the newly planned downtown central business district of Shenzhen, this project is located to the west and occupies two city blocks. It uses green space to separate itself off from the CBD and a residential area to the west. The mall provides a leisure shopping area for people from both these areas, while serving to attract visitors from elsewhere, thus stimulating the development of the district.

In organizing the spaces, the community park is used as a transitional area between the business functions of the complex. The whole site is developed in a 9 meter by 9 meter grid. In the center of the mall, a shopping street runs as an axis from south to north. Numerous pedestrian access routes reinforce the link between the two blocks.

Four design themes are employed in this project: a "country square", a "national garden", a "fantasy world", and a "pace of urban". These themes are combined with the functional spaces of shipping, exhibition, recreation, and bars, nightclub, and performance. Located to the east are a circular theater, a fun fair, recreation facilities, fountains, green spaces, small-scale architecture pieces, and sculptures.

Easy access is provided from both the west and the east. Stylized roofs are used on the buildings, which are mainly two-story, and weather shelter is provided. The general feeling is one of tranquillity and harmony.

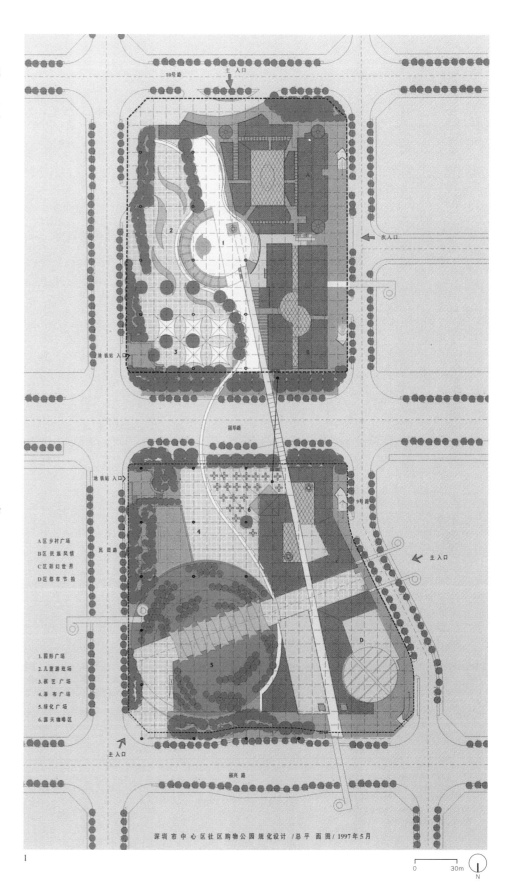

1 Master plan
Opposite:
    General view from south

1

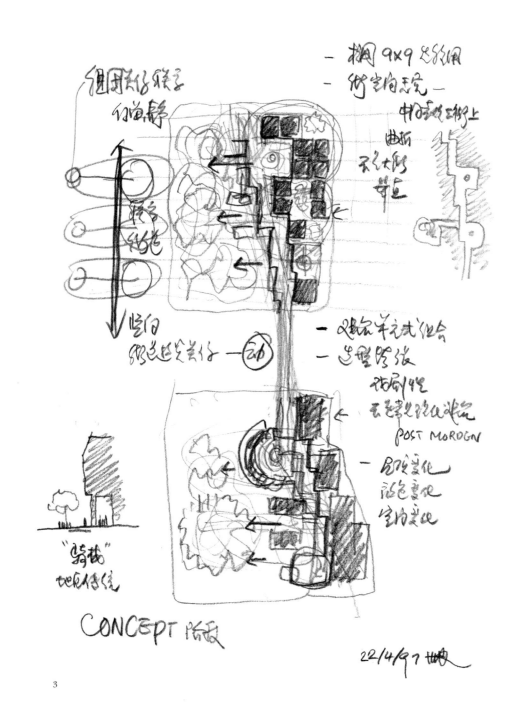

CONCEPT 階段

22/4/97 世民

3

4

5

6

International Conference and Exhibition Center

Competition 1997
Qingdao, China
Qingdao Municipal People's Government
Site area: 205,000 square meters
Total floor area: 86,500 square meters
Reinforced concrete, steel
Stone, curtain wall, metal panel

This project is located at one of the squares in the high-technology area of Qingdao. Five squares are linked by a 90-meter-wide green belt running south to north. Because the site is split into three sections by the pedestrian passage and visual corridor, the main building is located symmetrically on the axis and the supporting buildings are placed to the sides. The exhibition center contains a two-story-high exhibition hall with a capacity of 2,500 standard units. The conference hall is located on the top of the building, enabling it to share public facilities with the exhibition hall, providing for more efficient use of these facilities.

An oval plaza is created in the midst of the center by cutting 6 meters into the sloping site. The plaza draws the visitor to the reception hall, restaurant, and other public facilities. The slopes on each side cut through the overpasses to offer variations in elevation and this effect climaxes at the 90-meter-wide pedestrian passage. This allows for a connection of the five squares whilst maintaining respect for the visual perspective. Accordingly, this project becomes the bridge to these five squares.

A wide range of building materials are used according to the structure gradation in order to achieve a dynamic elevation. The roofs take the form of wave-like, light nets, so the building resembles a flying seabird, implying that this high-technology area is like a migratory bird on a journey. This offers food for the imagination and creates a unique visual effect.

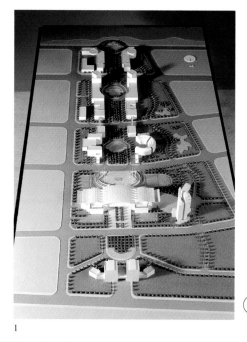

1

2

1 Model, showing site planning
2 Main view from south square
3 Ground level exhibition hall plan and
  conference hall plan

3

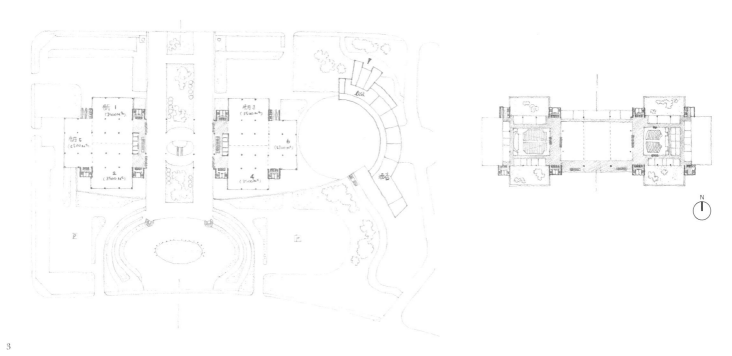

HOTELS

Nanhai Hotel

Design/Completion 1983/1985
Shekou, China
The Hong Kong Shanghai Bank Corporation Limited, China Merchants Holdings Co. Ltd,
Mirimar International Hotel Management Co., Bank of China Shenzhen Branch
Site area: 3,500 square meters
Total floor area: 43,100 square meters
Reinforced concrete
Stone, tile, glass, paint

With a backdrop of hills and facing the open sea, the Nanhai Hotel is located away from the city's busy traffic. The priority of the design is to ensure harmony between the hotel and its beautiful environment.

The master plan of the project is formed by five rectangular building blocks evenly distributed along a curved line that echoes the lines of the seashore and the hills. This provides hotel guests with sensational views of natural beauty. The main feature of the hotel buildings is their terraced forms, with each ascending floor set further back. This not only maximizes natural light and fresh air to the hotel rooms, but also harmonizes with the outline of the hill.

An overpass is placed between the main structure and the hill behind, while an artificial waterfall brings water to the lobby. These elements form a cohesive relationship between the buildings and the environment. Covered walkways and pavilions bridge the space between the sea and the main structure and around the swimming pool, creating an impression that the hotel extends to the water. The green space of the hotel blends with the foreshore vegetation to form a single open space. The hotel gate is placed on the hill side, preserving the tranquil and pleasant atmosphere of the seashore.

To gain the full benefit of the location, the ground level is raised so that visitors can enjoy the ocean view (with Hong Kong visible in the distance) from the lobby, cafe, restaurant, and other public spaces.

Other functions, such as the multi-function hall, recreation facilities, and service areas, are placed underground in order to maximize green space for the hotel.

The interior design is simple and fresh, using contemporary Chinese furniture, sculptures, and paintings. Uncomplicated and elegant materials are used on the floors and walls.

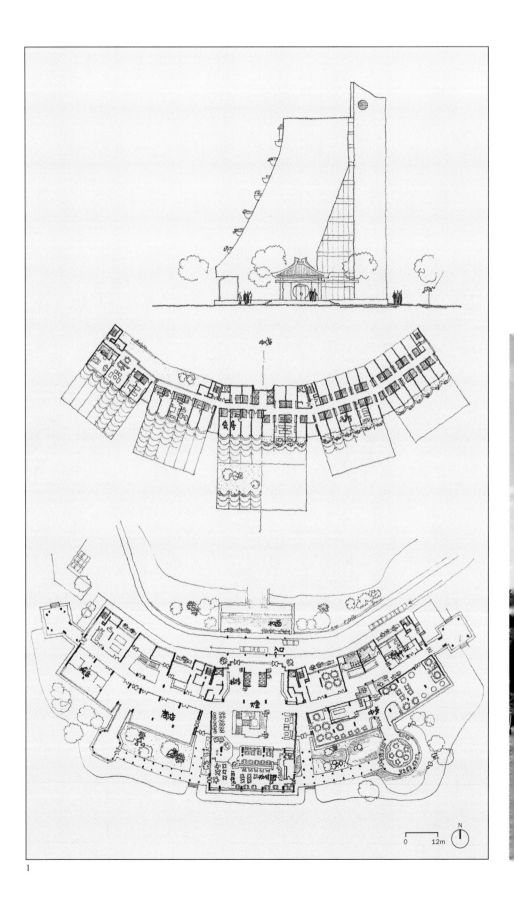

1

2

3　　　　　　　　　　　　　　　　　　　　　4

5

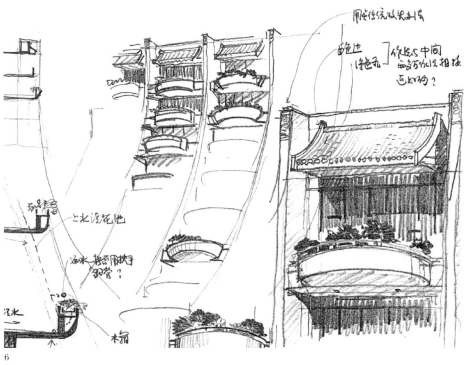

6

周围传统收泥封檐

铝板也
浮雕?

依檐口中间
无砌收檐招接
瓦利瓦?

と水浇花地

涵水 稳节围扶子
加管?

泥水

木箱

6   Study sketch of hotel room balconies
7&8   South elevation
9   Balcony detail
10   Concept sketch
11   Swimming pool and view through covered
       walkway to the sea

7

8

9

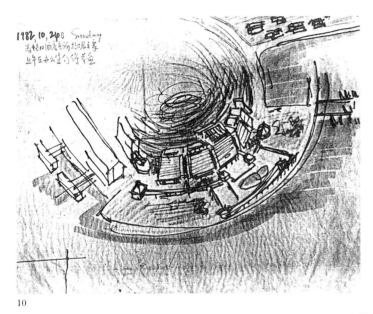

10

11

12

13

14

12   Study sketch of atrium
13   View of atrium and stair to basement level public area
14   View inside atrium looking east
15   General view of atrium

15

16

17

18

19

16   Sketch of Western-style restaurant
17   Interior view of Chinese restaurant
18   Entrance view of Chinese restaurant
19   Meeting, restaurant, and function room
20   Study sketch of restaurant interior
21   Interior of Chinese restaurant

20

21

22

23

24

25

22 Study sketch of guest room
23 Guest room
24 Guest suite
25 Presidential suite with Chinese-style interior decoration

Hotel Sinomonde

Design/Completion 1988/1991
Montreal, Canada
Gestion Sinomonde Inc.
Site area: 29,850 square meters
Total floor area: 30,000 square meters
Reinforced concrete, steel
Glazed tile, wall tile, glass, paint
In cooperation with Jacques Beique Architect, Montreal (Canada)

The hotel is located at the intersection of two main streets at the south end of Montreal's Chinatown. It faces the famous cultural and tourist district, with government offices and busy commercial areas at its back.

Due to council restrictions, the building height was limited to eight stories. Escalators lead from the west-facing entrance through a grand garden-like atrium space on the second floor. The atrium contains streams and bridges and is surrounded by Chinese and Western-style restaurants, a bar, a coffee bar, and a conference hall, creating a flowing, lively and warm public space. This is an ideal indoor environment for Montreal's long and extremely cold winters.

The bright colors and bold outlines of Chinese architecture are used to emphasize the hotel's cultural origins. The rooftop, eaves, and corridors all display Chinese characteristics, forming a sharp contrast to modern Western high-rise buildings. Chinese culture is also reflected in the interior design and the furniture, emphasizing the history of Montreal's Chinatown and creating a symbolic link with China itself.

1

2

1   Study sketch of elevation
2   General view from southeast
3   Study sketch of balconies
4   South elevation showing traditional Chinese character of the rooftop and balconies

72

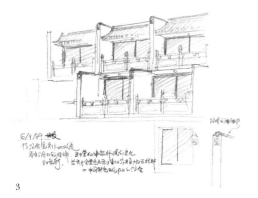

3

4

5

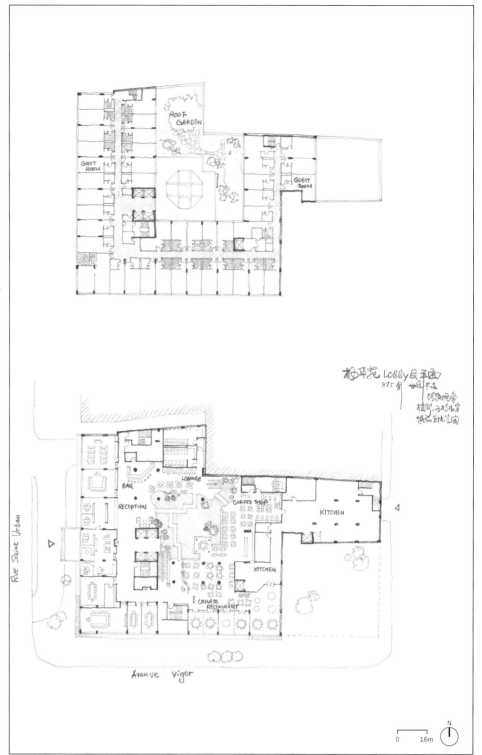

6

7

5 Entrance
6 First floor plan (below) and
  guest room plan (above)
7 Reception counter
8 Public corridor and reception counter

9

9　Western-style restaurant opening onto the
　　atrium garden
10　Sketch of view from lift lobby
11　Study sketch of the atrium
12　Atrium view showing Chinese garden

10

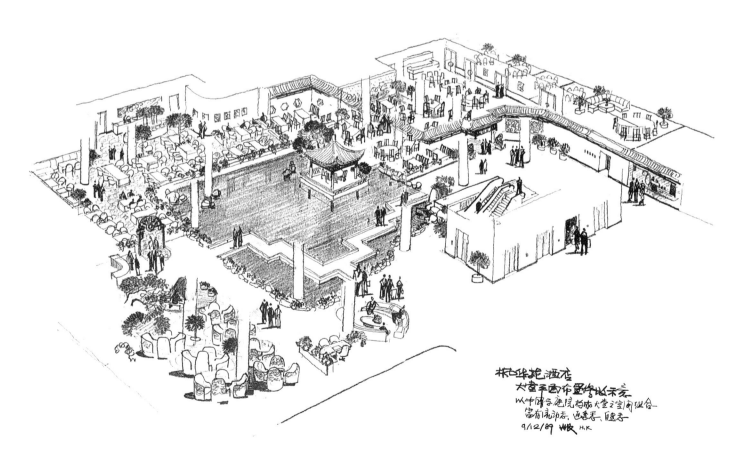

林华地酒店
大堂平面布置修地示意
以中国子庭院环境特点、大堂之空间组合
富有流动态、迂迷着、回里态
9/12/89 州版 H.K

11

12

13   Sitting area of guest room
14   Guest room interior, finished in light colors
15   Guest suite, finished in traditional Chinese colors

13

14

15

Qin Xing Hotel

Design 1986
Xian, China
Qin Xing Hotel Development Ltd
Site area: 7,500 square meters
Total floor area: 42,000 square meters
Reinforced concrete
Glass, tile, stone
In cooperation with China Northwest Building Design & Research Institute

Xian is one of the most famous ancient cities of China. This hotel meets the city's need to accommodate a growing number of overseas tourists. The municipal government wanted a high-rise building that would create a distinctive feature on the city's skyline; the hotel management wanted more hotel and public space to accommodate the large number of tourist groups, and additional facilities for evening activities.

To satisfy these requirements, and to comply with an overall height limit of 20 stories, the plan incorporates two tower structures of different heights. The taller tower houses hotel rooms, while the smaller tower houses the hotel's central activity space—an eight-story atrium surrounded by multi-function halls, restaurants, and bars.

The height variation of the two towers provides a range of distinctive elevations from different angles. The majority of hotel rooms are oriented to avoid the hot summer sun and cold winter winds.

The quadrangle shape and sloping roof of the main tower create a sense of verticality. Simple rectangular windows and limited use of glass curtain walls provide an uncomplicated and clear outlook. The glazed roof tiles used for the pavilions and lower level buildings respond to the climate and architecture of the Xian region.

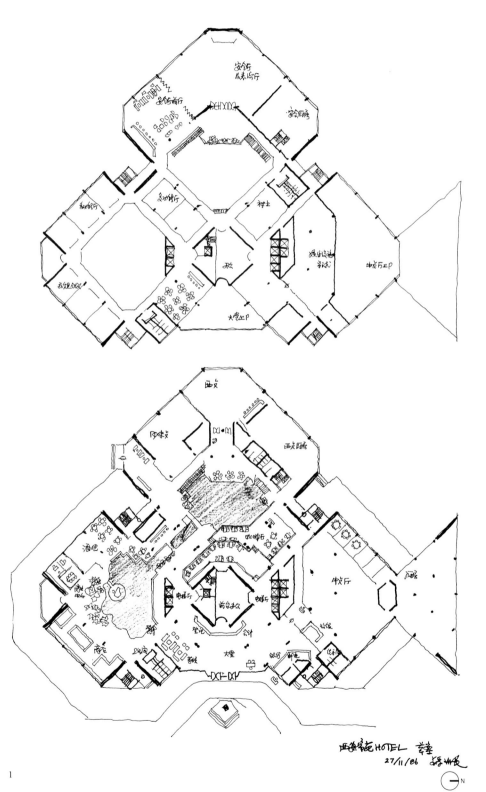

1

2

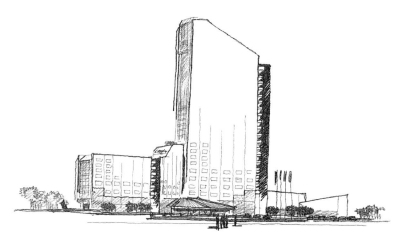

3

4

Mingru Hotel

Schematic & preliminary design 1992
Beihai, China
Thai-China (Beihai) Property Investment Co. Ltd
Site area: 20,080 square meters
Total floor area: 52,277 square meters
Reinforced concrete
Stone, glass, wall tile

The hotel is located at the beach of Beihai, which is famous in Guangxi Province (in southern China) for its sunshine and scenery. The neighboring area forms a peninsula. It is an ideal hotel site. The objective of the master plan is to maximize the ocean frontage so the beach can be used for swimming and other activities. The 16-story hotel tower is V-shaped, giving each room its own view of the sea. The other main functions—the lobby, restaurant, recreation areas, and lifts—are placed at the front of the hotel to take advantage of the views.

To cater for the business and social activities of guests, a conference and recreation center and a banquet hall are located to one side of the main structure.

The hotel is a typical piece of beach architecture. The facade is composed of simple and lively white walls and gray windows, which complement the blue sea, green lawns, and colorful gardens.

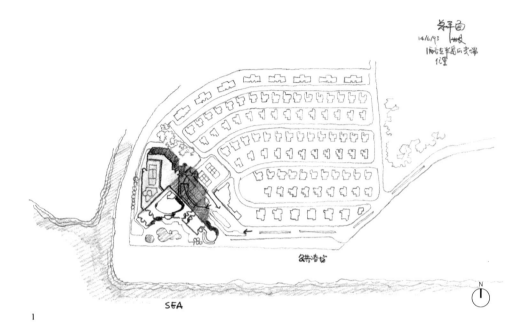

1

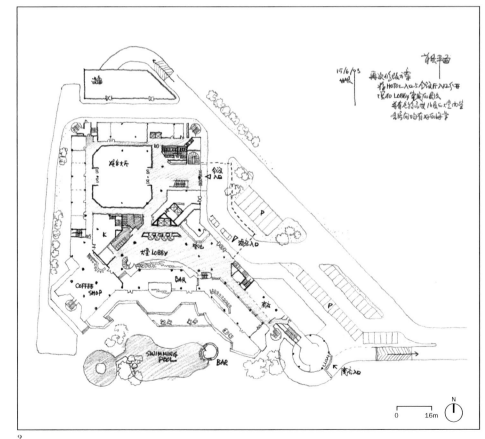

2

1 Site plan
2 Ground level plan
3 Second level plan
4 Study sketch showing sea views
5 View from the sea

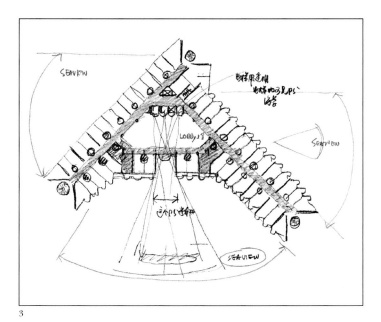

3

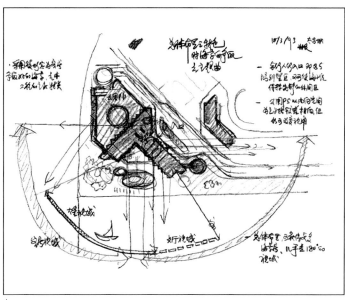

4

5

Baofa Building

Preliminary design 1992
Shenzhen, China
Shenzhen Development Bank Ltd
Site area: 6,370 square meters
Total floor area: 51,460 square meters
Concrete frame
Glass, stone, metal panel

The building is located in the developing area of Shenzhen. The client required a complex incorporating hotel, commercial office, and banking functions, to improve the level of services in the area. At the same time, the client desired a tall and magnificent hall within the building to provide a special attraction. This hall, together with the wide pedestrian square in front of the building, serves as the activity center. This design constitutes a major revision of the initial design proposal originally provided by Peddle Thorp Architects.

1

2

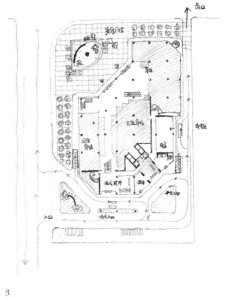

3

4

0   16m

N

1   Sketch of street elevation
2   Aerial view of model
3   Ground level plan
4   Main lobby level plan

Well Bond Grand Hotel

Design 1993
Shenzhen, China
Well Bond Group Ltd
Site area: 9,612 square meters
Total floor area: 109,880 square meters
Reinforced concrete
Stone, curtain wall, metal panel

This hotel is situated on the side of Lichee Lake in the financial district of Shenzhen, combining an excellent central location with a valuable natural environment. The client wished to develop a five-star duplex hotel.

The master plan takes into account wider issues of urban space planning and emphasizes integration with the natural environment. In accordance with the client's preferences, curved and circular shapes are the dominant architectural forms.

A circular open plaza, which echoes the curved shape of the hotel tower, is placed at the intersection of two main streets, serving as the starting point in a sequence of architectural spaces. The circular and semicircular podium and tower are positioned at the lakeside, enjoying spectacular views.

A Classical European architectural language is used in the design of the three sections of building elevation, pillared arches, Roman-style colonnade, and framed doors and windows.

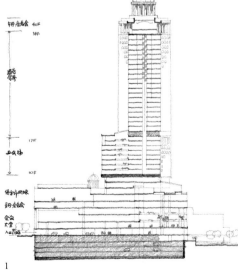

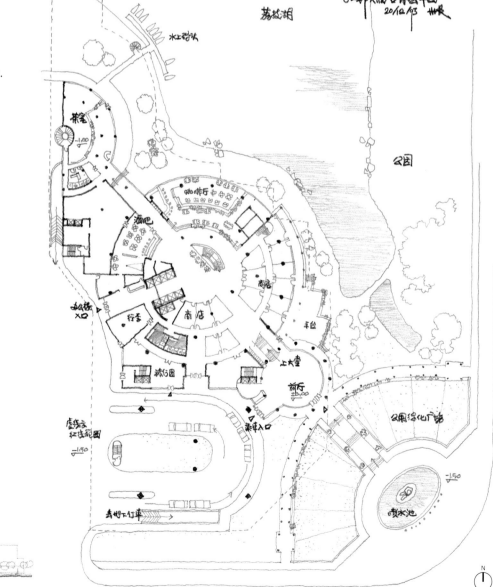

1

2

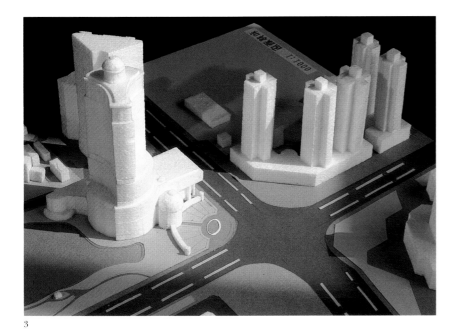

1 Section
2 Ground floor plan
3 Aerial view of model from south
4 General view from southeast showing
   the lakeside location

3

4

Shanglong Building

Design/Completion 1994/1999
Shenzhen, China
Shanglong Investment Co. Ltd
Site area: 6,134 square meters
Total floor area: 8,213 square meters
Steel, reinforced concrete
Stone, curtain wall, metal panel
Winning international competition entry

The site is a narrow terrace on the main street of Shenzhen. The design brief called for a building complex housing a five-star hotel, offices, and retail, as well as the transformation of an existing small open space and public refuse station into a pleasant urban green park.

The design uses regular rows of columns, a long, narrow ornamental pool, paving, and tall coconut trees to link the park with the building.

A square is located in front of the hotel to aid circulation on the narrow site. Internally, an atrium provides a central public space and gives access to the various functions of the complex. Offices and apartments are located on the upper floors, affording views of the newly created park.

The building's elevation has a Classical European style, in keeping with the historical nature of the surrounding Luohu district. The Shanglong Building is a distinctive addition to the Shenzhen skyline.

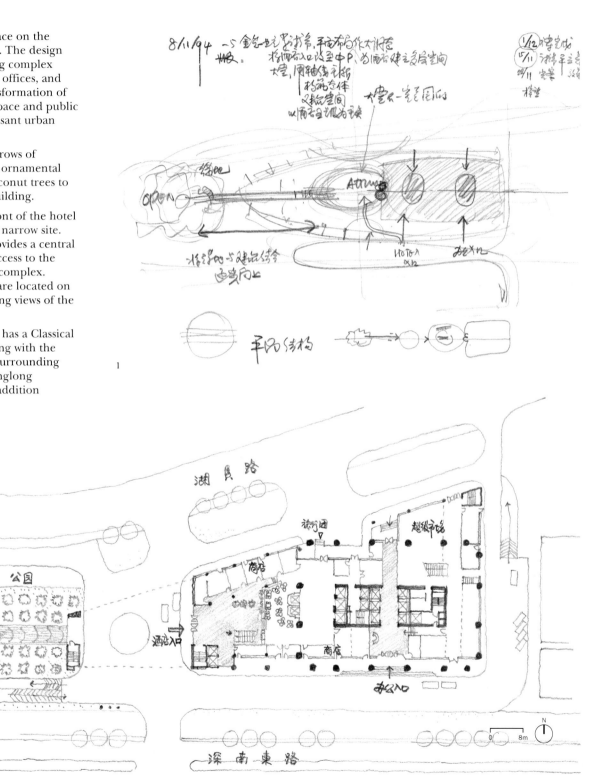

1

2

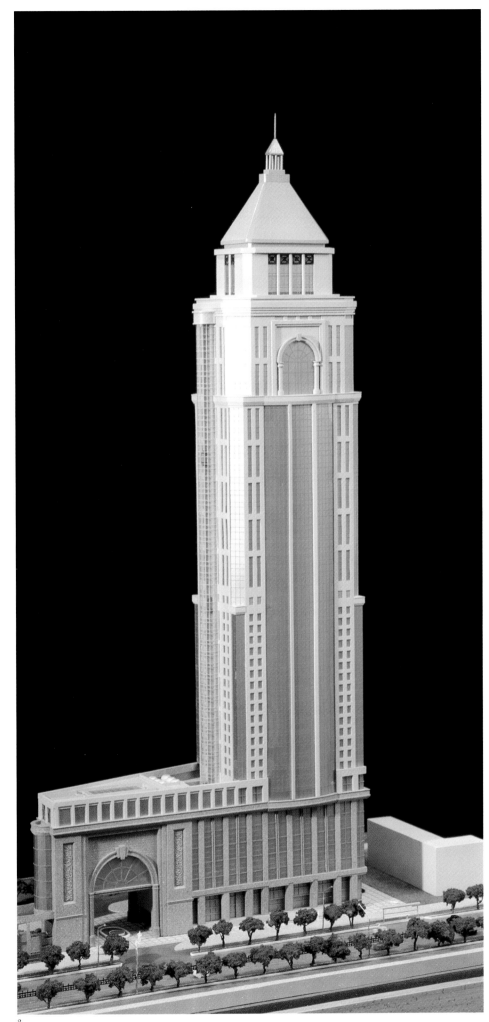

3

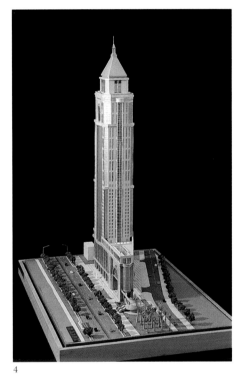

4

1   Concept sketch
2   Master plan
3   General view of model from south
4   View from west of main city street

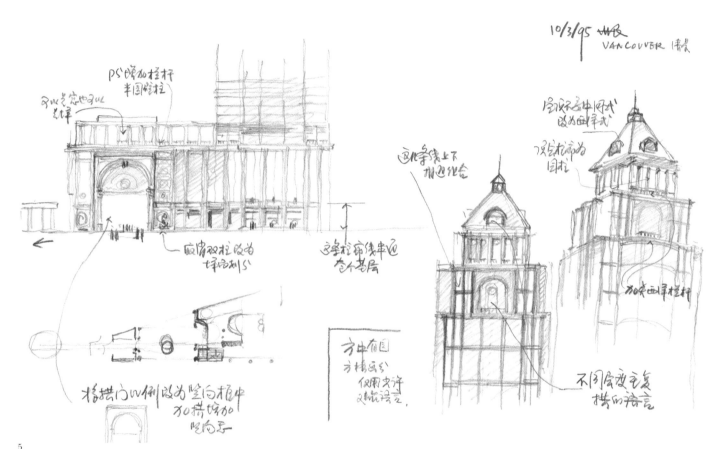

5

6

7

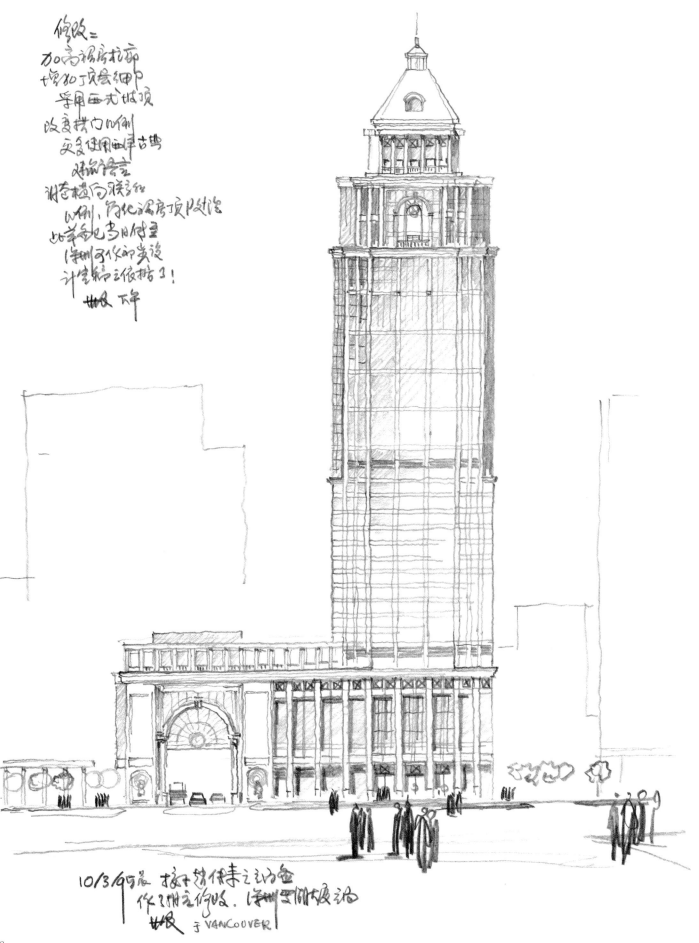

Imperial Capital Hotel

Design 1991
Louyang, China
Site area: 8,000 square meters
Total floor area: 35,000 square meters
Concrete
Stone, tile, glass, roof tile, wood

The project is to be built in Louyang, one of China's ancient capitals. The master plan comprises a triangular-shaped main tower with a hexagonal podium. In front of the hotel building, a six-story-high atrium is created by using the setback rooftop structure. Three elevators rise through the atrium, affording views over the ancient city of Louyang.

The main activity space of the hotel extends from the atrium to the Imperial Garden, where green space, pavilions, flowing water, and colorful plantings are enclosed by a perimeter wall. The main building structure combines two extended wings in a grand and imperial gesture. Elements of traditional Chinese architecture are used to ensure the building is in sympathy with its regional context.

1

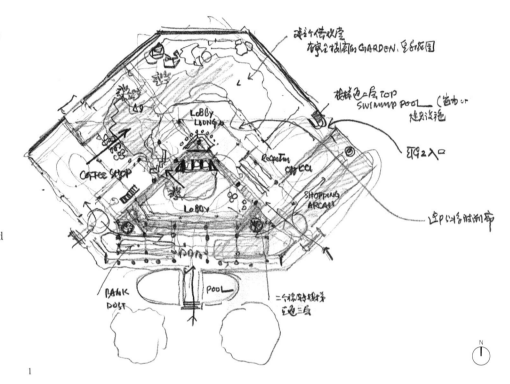

2

1   Sketch plan of lobby level
2   Aerial view of model
3   View from west
4   Elevation sketch
5   General view from south

3

4

5

Qilin Resort

Design/Completion 1995/1997
Shenzhen, China
Shenzhen Urban Planning & Land Administration Bureau
Site area: 12,000 square meters
Total floor area: 5,830 square meters
Reinforced concrete
Stone, glass, paint

Qilin Resort is a villa area located in a suburb of Shenzhen and is to be used by distinguished visitors from the municipal government. It consists of five villas at the foot of the city hills, each with a separate garden and private space. The architect was commissioned to design the largest of these villas, which faces a lake. It contains 38 luxury rooms and suites and also a presidential suite and corresponding office facilities. From the hall of the villa, and from the host room, guest rooms, dining room, and meeting room, visitors will get the sense that they are surrounded by hills and floating on the lake.

The ground floor is used as rooms for the entourage and for the swimming pool. The second floor houses the presidential suite and banquet room. The third floor houses the recreation facilities. Separate entrances are provided for visitors and VIPs. The interior design is European in style.

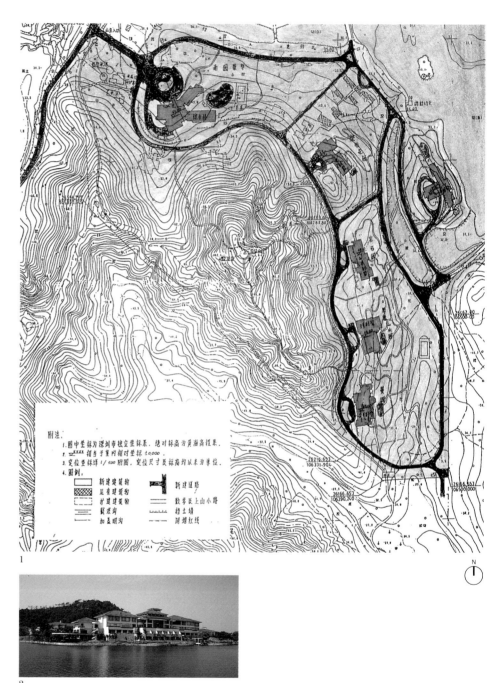

1

2

3

4

7

5

6

1 Master plan
2&3 Overall view of resort from northeast
4 View of Building 1
5 Roof detail
6 Lower level facade detail
7 South elevation

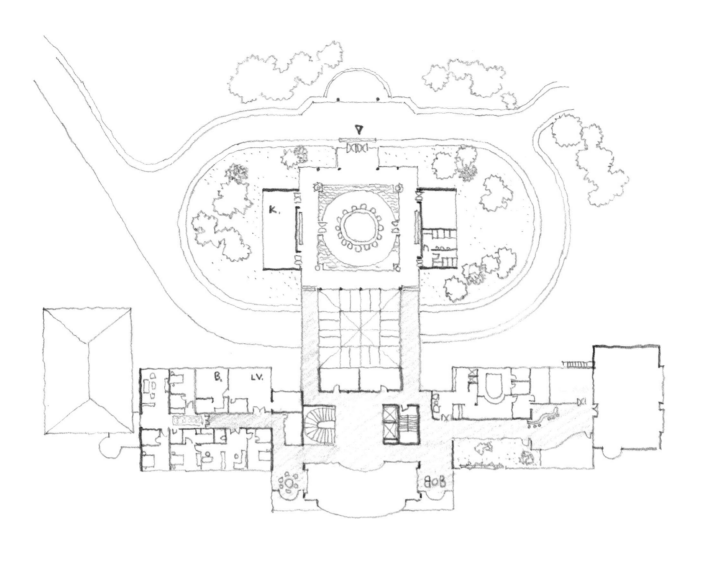

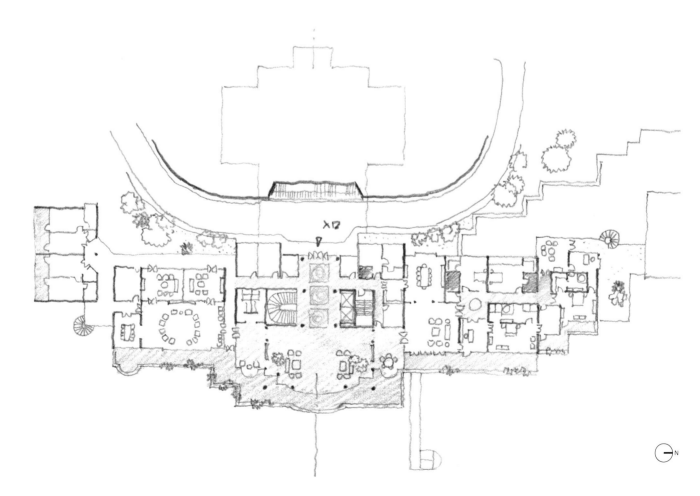

8   Building 1: main lobby and VIP suite plan
9&10 View of entrance
11   View of main lobby from front court of VIP suite
12   Aerial view of main lobby

9

10

11

12

13

14

15

16

17

13 Conference hall
14 Living room of VIP suite
15 Dining hall
16 Master bedroom in VIP suite
17 Swimming pool

State Guest House

Competition 1996
Shenzhen, China
Shenzhen Urban Planning & Land Administration Bureau
Site area: 47,000 square meters
Total floor area: 29,000 square meters
Reinforced concrete
Stone, curtain wall, metal panel

The project is situated to the west of downtown Futian, at the northwest corner of the Shenzhen Golf Course, near a main section of the Shenzhen–Shennan Road. As a center where high-ranking foreign officials and distinguished guests are received by the Shenzhen municipal government, and also as a place to stage grand celebrations, it is essential that the complex displays elegance both in the arrangement of interior and exterior spaces and in the design of the buildings themselves.

Facing the main road, the 17-story guest house serves as the focus. Its symmetrical plan evokes a sense of grandeur. On the third floor of the podium, elongated to form the focus of the east elevation, a 1,000-seat banquet hall faces downtown Shenzhen. Each building in the complex is arranged with strict symmetry on its axes, and is designed to make an impressive architectural statement. The golf course to the west and south provides a green, park-like setting for the multi-story buildings.

The elevation reveals a series of ascending floors interspersed with glass, achieving a marriage of traditional Chinese and modern architecture.

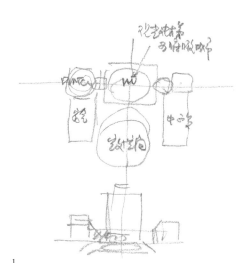

1

1 Concept study sketch
2 Aerial view of model showing layout
3 Elevation detail study
4 Sketch of main tower
5 View from north square

2

100

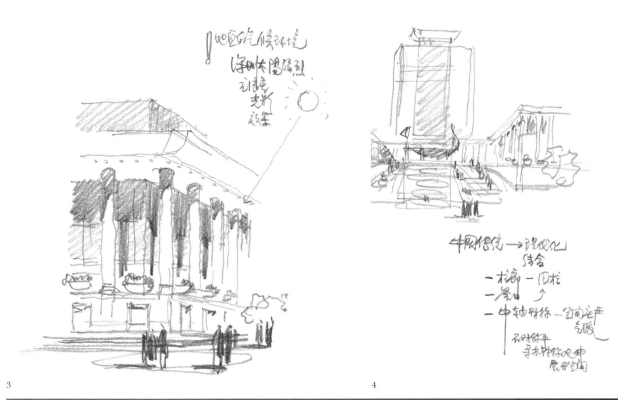

3

4

5

6

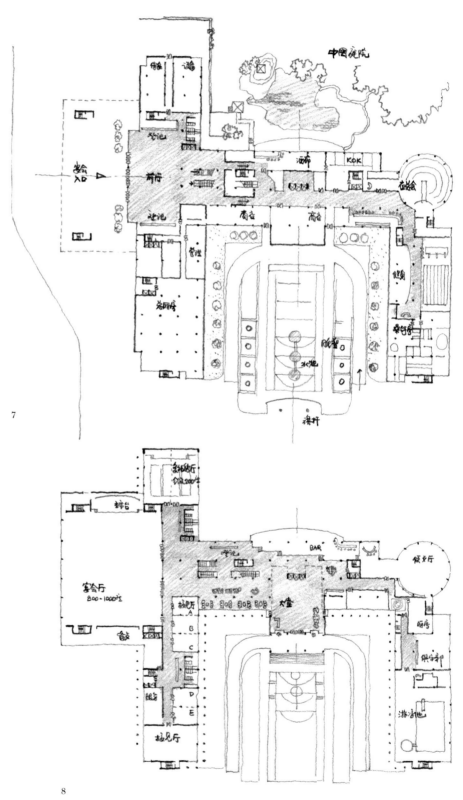

7

8

6   Model view from south garden
7   Ground level plan showing banquet hall entrance
8   Main lobby and banquet hall plan
9   Model view showing central square for state guests
10   Aerial view from north axis

9

10

COMPLEX
BUILDINGS

Tianan International Building

Design/Completion 1988/1993
Shenzhen, China
Tianan China Investments Co. Ltd
Site area: 5,948 square meters
Total floor area: 91,000 square meters
Reinforced concrete
Curtain wall, tile, metal panel
In cooperation with China Electronics Eng. Design Institute
Winning international competition entry

This project forms part of a group of high-rise buildings located in the most sought-after section of Shenzhen. It is a luxury complex consisting of a hotel, offices, apartments, department stores, and a multi-function hall.

Due to restrictions governing sight lines, and the requirement for a multi-function hall within the complex, it was necessary to create a traffic "corridor" for north–south motor vehicle circulation. This arrangement also provides an independent entrance/exit for each component of the building.

The lobby is located on the ground floor. The department stores are located in the section of greatest commercial value—the section facing the street—thus providing maximum exposure to passers-by.

The structure of the building is an 8 meter by 8 meter grid of columns, allowing flexibility in the design of the offices, apartments, the hotel (on the upper levels of the podium), and the tower.

The unique U-shaped plan of the tower is generated by semicircular and rectangular shapes which overlap and extend into each other. This generates a cohesive relationship with the existing high-rise buildings. The curved golden-glazed curtain wall and the pink facade with protruding windows create contrasts in form, volume, and color with the existing, relatively monotonous, buildings in the neighborhood.

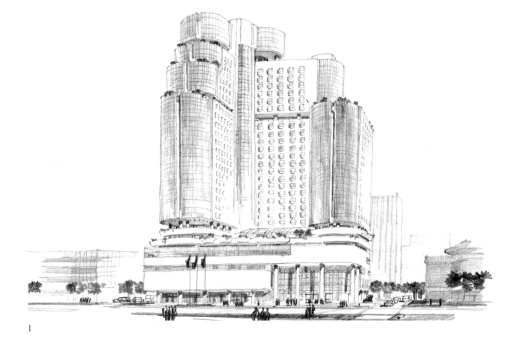

1

2

1   General sketch
2   Night view from south
3   General view from south

3

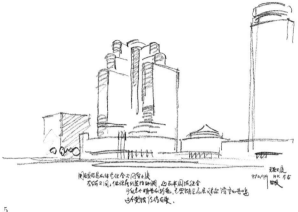

4 Elevation of curtain wall and windows
5 Study sketch of elevation
6 Window detail
7 Elevation from west
8 Section

4

6

7

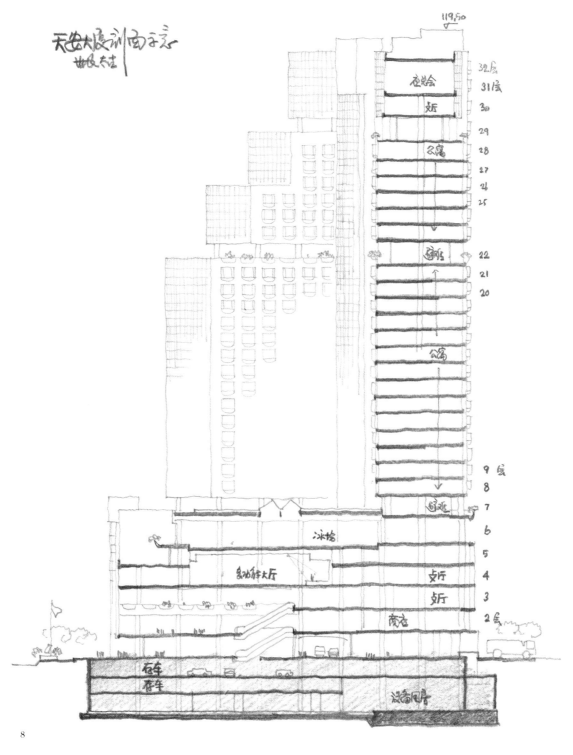

天安大厦剖面图
世貿大厦

119.50

座谈会 32层
31层
弘 30
29
公寓 28
27
26
25
22
设施 21
20
公寓
9 层
8
设施 7
冰坡 6
5
多功能大厅 文厅 4
弘 3
商店 2 层
石车
存车
设备间层

9 Three-story commercial space
10 Concept sketches
11 View of commercial space

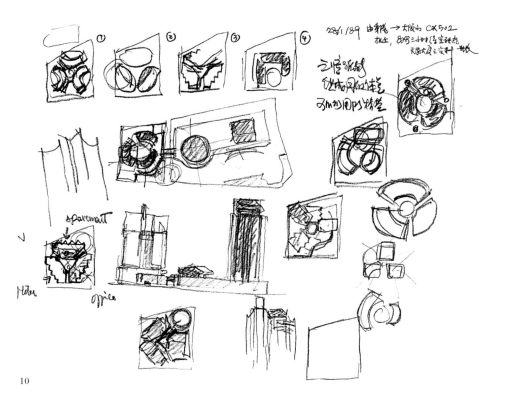

10

11

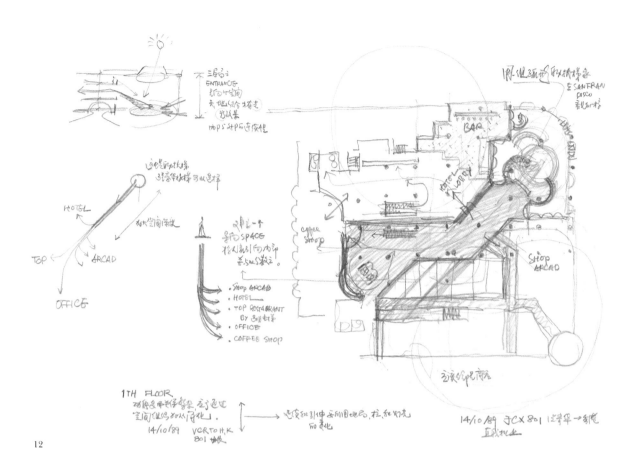

12

13

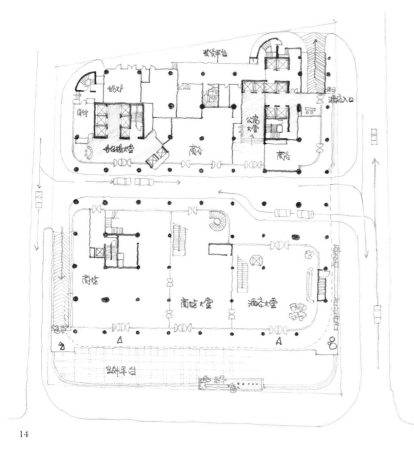

14

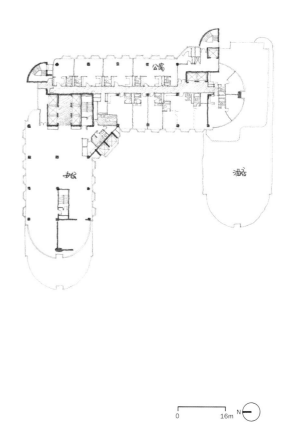

15

16

12 Concept sketches
13 Interior of coffee shop
14 Ground floor plan (left) and upper floor plan (right)
15 Interior of ballroom
16 Interior of club restaurant at the top of the building

International Trade Plaza

Design/Completion 1990/1996
Shenzhen, China
Shenzhen Properties & Resources Development (Group) Ltd
Site area: 3,767 square meters
Total floor area: 70,000 square meters
Reinforced concrete
Stone, curtain wall, tile

The project is located in one of the most expensive areas of Shenzhen. To fully utilize the site potential and improve the existing architectural environment, a purpose-built 35-story apartment building was created. Four existing blocks—containing the International Trading Building, Tianan Plaza, the Trade Commerce Building, and an apartment building—were combined by means of a four-level podium, creating a new building complex.

The ground level of the podium is built on stilts in order to leave space for the existing roads and traffic as well as providing access to the underground car parks associated with the existing buildings. The main section of the new complex, the central square, is placed on the second level, where it can be easily accessed from all areas. The four-level atrium, which is naturally lit through a glass roof, creates an ideal environment for restaurants, snack counters, coffee shops, and bars.

The completion of the International Trade Plaza has dramatically improved traffic flow in the district, as well as providing the biggest downtown shopping complex in Shenzhen.

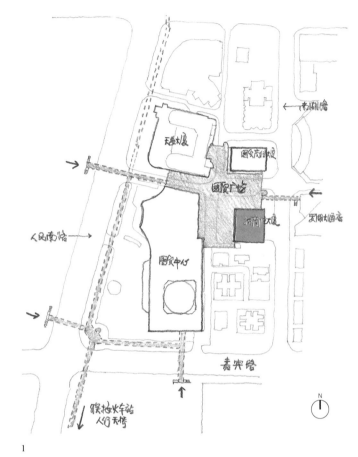

1

1 Site plan
2 Aerial view of model from west showing the four existing buildings
3 Street view from south

2

Huafu Center

Competition 1992
Fuzhou, China
Huafu Investment Co. Ltd
Site area: 18,834 square meters
Total floor area: 179,000 square meters
Concrete
Curtain wall, metal panel, stone
Winning competition entry

This project is situated in the busy commercial center of Fuzhou. The 68-story complex houses bank offices, a luxury hotel, and apartments, along with a shopping mall and recreation, restaurant, and other facilities.

A spacious public square with a well-planned green area is placed in front of the building to enhance the pedestrian experience. Because the site is T-shaped, a tall, wide entrance is used to attract people to the shopping mall at the rear. This layout is a highly efficient utilization of the available space.

The outstanding feature of the project is its simple elevated form. A rooftop garden and two glass elevators offer a bird's-eye view of the city. As the tallest building in the neighborhood, Huafu Center will quickly become a tourist attraction.

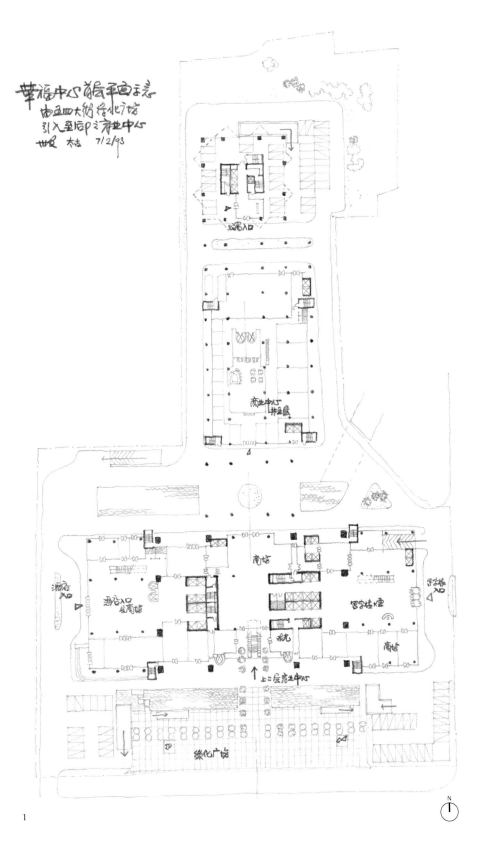

1   Ground level plan
2   View of model from public square
3   Concept sketch
4   Perspective showing the architectural style

2

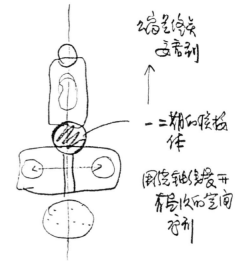

3

4

International Science and Technology Building

Design/Completion 1991/1996
Shenzhen, China
Shenzhen North Engineering Development Co.
Site area: 9,927 square meters ·
Total floor area: 60,000 square meters
Reinforced concrete
Stone, glass, metal panel
In cooperation with Mechanical Electron Industry Ministry and
Engineering Design Research Institute, Shenzhen Branch (China)

The main theme of the design is the ancient Chinese belief that the universe consists of the round sky and the square earth, with four directions and eight dimensions. The tower is composed of two cubes twisted to an angle of 45 degrees. Octagonal structures protrude from the flat building facades.

The design creates a clear separation between the tower and the podium. A four-story-high shared space is placed between the commercial space and the tower. This space is connected with the outside scenery through the three-story-high glass walls of the atrium.

The cantilever structure of the tower is supported by eight columns at intervals of 8 meters, and is capped by an independent circular rotating restaurant at the top.

The building's clean "sliced" elevation and sectional variations create a sophisticated appearance that reflects modern advances in science and technology.

1

1   General view sketch
2   West view of city skyline showing scale and context
3   Night view

2

3

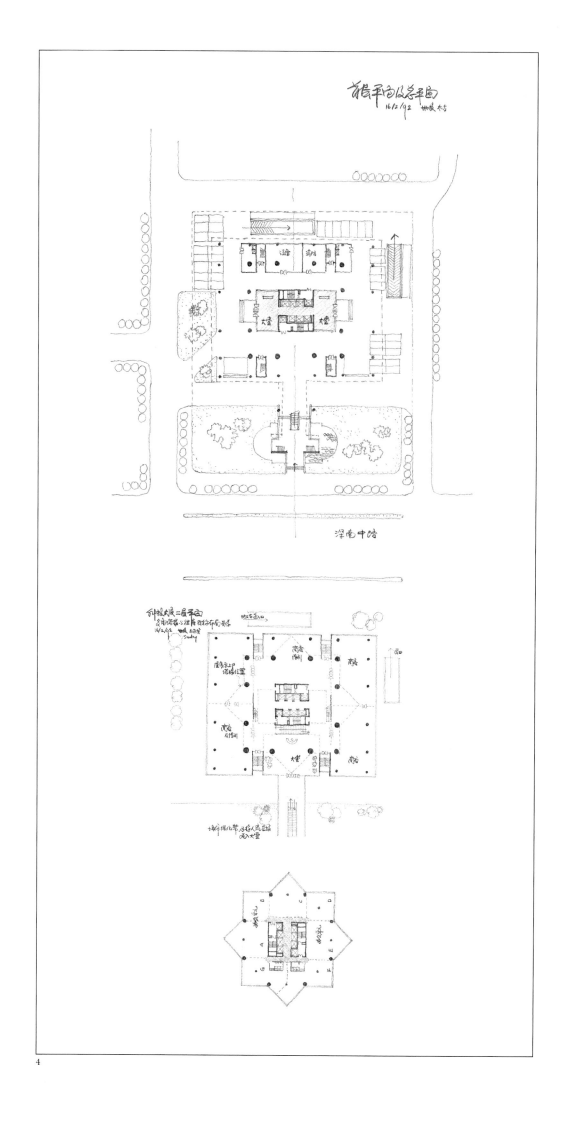

附38層的推進平台
再次用筆法勾画相對关係
9/7/91 略   設文中央病院

4 Ground level plan (above), podium plan
  (middle), tower plan (below)
5 Study sketch of elevation
6 View showing glass and metal panel exterior

5

6

Hua Du Garden

Design/Completion 1988/1993
Shenzhen, China
China National Native Produce & Animal Byproducts Import & Export Co.
Site area: 4,819 square meters
Total floor area: 42,000 square meters
Reinforced concrete
Tile, curtain wall

The project is located at the corner of two main roads in the Shenzhen CBD. To fulfill the client's request that the main entrance face the intersection, the design comprises two rectangular office blocks centered on a three-story atrium.

Spaces for business activities, exhibitions, and conferences are placed around the atrium, which also accommodates the main entrance.

The towers are capped with quarter-circle glass curtain walls oriented in opposite directions. From the luxury offices within, there are sweeping views over Shenzhen city towards Hong Kong. These curtain walls, and the windows in the building facade, recall the shape of a traditional Chinese fan, symbolizing the trading activities of the client.

1 Concept sketch of plan
2 Study sketch featuring original concept based on the shape of a traditional Chinese fan
3 Window detail
Opposite:
   Street view from southwest

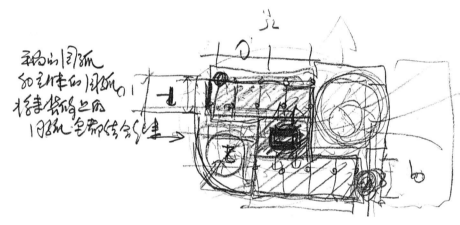

1

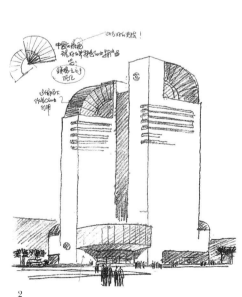

2

3

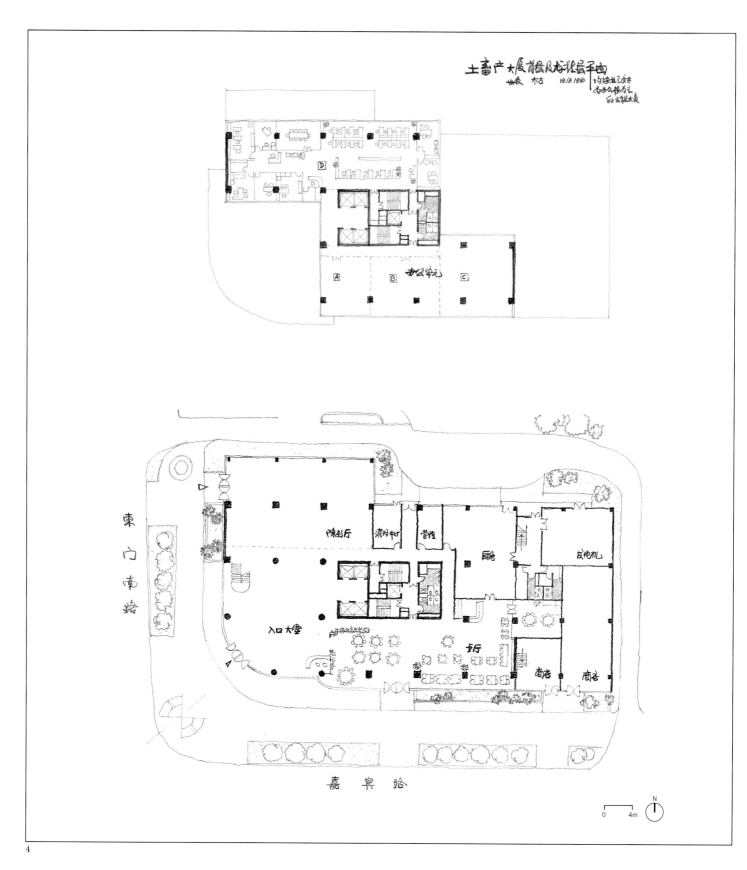

土畜产大厦首层及标准层平面
冊友 太占 12/8/88 约议址位置由
有两条限边车
而亚建大厦

陳列厅 消防中心 管理 厨房 发电机

入口大堂 大厅 商店 商店

東门南路

嘉宾路

0 4m N

5

6

7

4 Ground level plan (below) and mid-rise office level plan (above)
5&6 Shop at the second level
7 Interior of three-story atrium space

Shum Yip Building

Design/Completion 1992/1995
Haerbin, China
Shum Yip Properties Development Co. Ltd
Site area: 2,394 square meters
Total floor area: 40,000 square meters
Reinforced concrete
Glass, stone, tile
In cooperation with Architecture Design Institute of Heilongjing (China)

This project combines commercial space, a hotel, apartments, offices, a restaurant, and recreation facilities in a 31-story structure—the tallest building in the city.

On the corner site, a small pedestrian square is place in front of the main building to separate pedestrian and vehicle traffic and enhance the city environment. The podium is used for commercial space; the tower contains hotel rooms in the center section, apartments and offices in the upper section, and a rotating restaurant on the top.

Within the podium, the public spaces are enclosed to provide relief from Haerbin's cold winters. The lower parts of the building have solid walls, while the upper parts have a glass curtain wall. The colors provided by the lighting endow the building with a light and lively atmosphere.

1   Sketch view from main street
2   Detail of south elevation
3   Site plan
4   View from south street

1

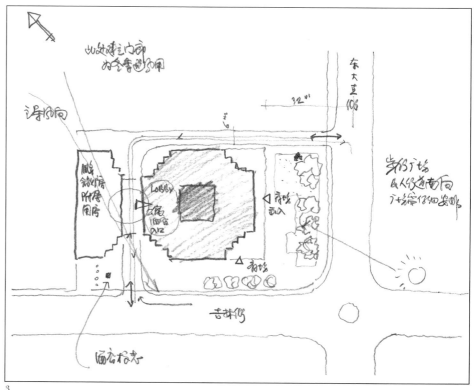

2

3

4

Huamin Plaza

Design/Completion 1991/1995
Shenzhen, China
Shum Yip Properties Development Co. Ltd
Site area: 2,529 square meters
Total floor area: 23,700 square meters
Reinforced concrete
Tile, glass, stone

Huamin Plaza is located about 200 meters from Luohu Railway Station, the main gateway between mainland China and Hong Kong. It is one of the busiest districts in Shenzhen.

Due to the limited site area, a cantilevered building structure is adopted, using a column grid of 6 meters by 8 meters. This leaves more room at the ground level for pedestrian circulation.

The lift core is placed at the center of the building, which permits flexible floor plans for office, hotel, and apartment use.

A multi-level podium is located at the lower levels to provide additional retail space in what is an extremely crowded area of the city.

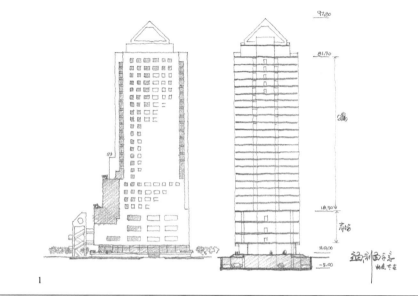

1

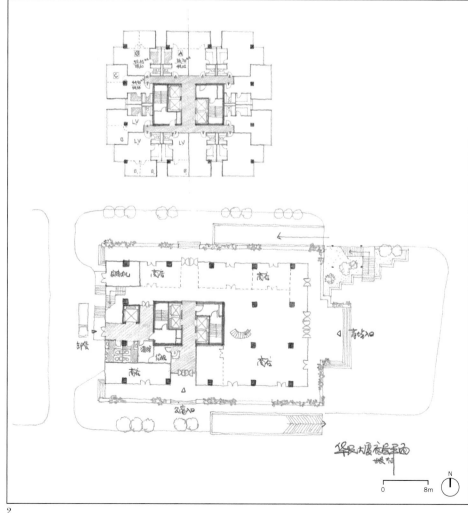

1   Elevation sketch
2   Site plan (below) and apartment level plan (above)
3   Southeast elevation

2

Hualu Chuanglu International Building

Competition 1992
Jinan, China
Qilu Construction Group Co.
Site area: 17,000 square meters
Total floor area: 172,345 square meters
Reinforced concrete
Stone, curtain wall, metal panel

This proposed skyscraper is located at the main intersection in the CBD of Jinan in eastern China. The 68-story high-rise complex is designed to accommodate a finance center, commercial offices, a hotel, apartments, conference facilities, and retail.

The master plan takes full advantage of the site and its surrounding traffic flows. Separate entrances are provided to all components of the complex, and pedestrian and vehicle circulation is clearly delineated to achieve maximum transport efficiency.

A Chinese pagoda design principle is applied in the hierarchical arrangement of office, apartment, and hotel spaces. In addition, consideration is given to the building elevation to ensure that the various sections are fully integrated into a single, modern architectural form.

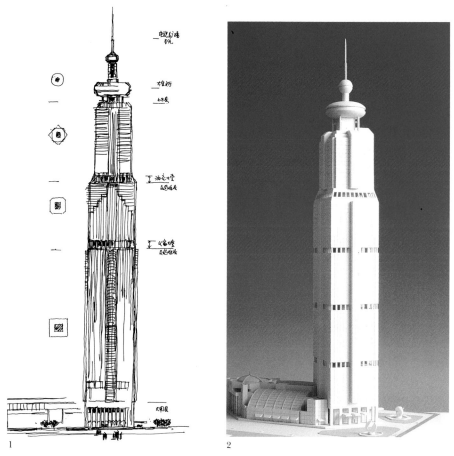

1

2

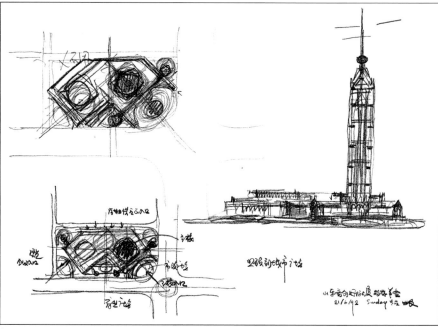

3

1   Elevation sketch
2   Model view showing the conceptual link
    with the Chinese pagoda
3   Initial concept sketches

International Commercial and Residential Building

Design/Completion 1986/1988
Shenzhen, China
Shenzhen Properties & Resources Development (Group) Ltd
Site area: 2,680 square meters
Total floor area: 23,000 square meters
Reinforced concrete
Glass, tile

The site is in the central part of the city. The project is designed for a number of small and middle-sized companies in the early stages of their growth. The central design concept was to create units of 71 to 119 square meters which would function as offices, reception spaces, meeting rooms, and residences. Where necessary, two or three units could be combined to form larger spaces. This unit concept is widely used in the architect's later projects.

1

1　General view from north
2&3　Interior view of office units

2　　　　　　　　　　　　　　　　3

Hongji Commercial Center

Schematic & preliminary design/Completion 1994/1999
Tianjin, China
Beiyang (Tianjin) Materials Group Co. Ltd
Site area: 10,388 square meters
Total floor area: 151,624 square meters
Reinforced concrete
Stone, curtain wall, metal panel
In cooperation with Tianjin Municipal Engineering Design & Research Institute (China)
Winning international competition entry

The aim of the design is to transform the site and its surroundings to create a new urban space by introducing new built objects. The client requested a new building complex providing offices, a hotel, conference centers, restaurants, and associated functions, in order to meet local demand in Tianjin. It was also important that the new buildings relate to the existing architecture in the surrounding precinct.

The site is well located in Tianjin city, within a scenic environment. The main entry road runs in a north-facing curve to take advantage of the city view. Three sides of the site are bounded by one-way streets, and there is no parking area. To overcome this problem, a traffic square is created at the ground level to separate pedestrians and vehicles. It is this consideration which gives the design its unique character.

The master plan makes provision for the future development of an underground railway station. Access to the station is via the podium, minimizing interference with the main complex.

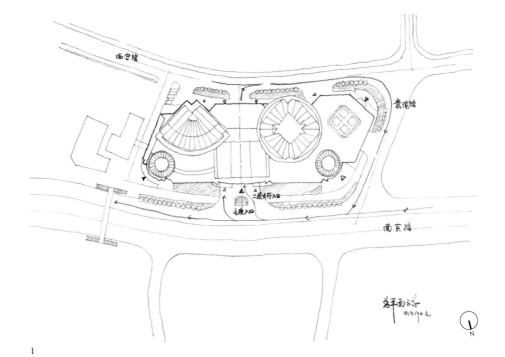

1

2

1   Master plan
2   Model view
3   General view from north

3

4   Concept sketch
5   Ground floor plan (below) and tower floor plan (above)
6   Study sketch of street elevation
7   Model view showing top of towers
8   Elevation sketch
9   Street view of model

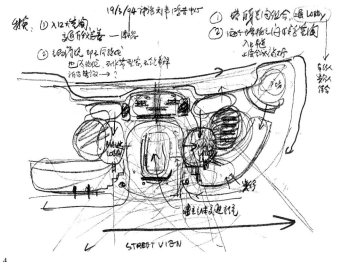

4

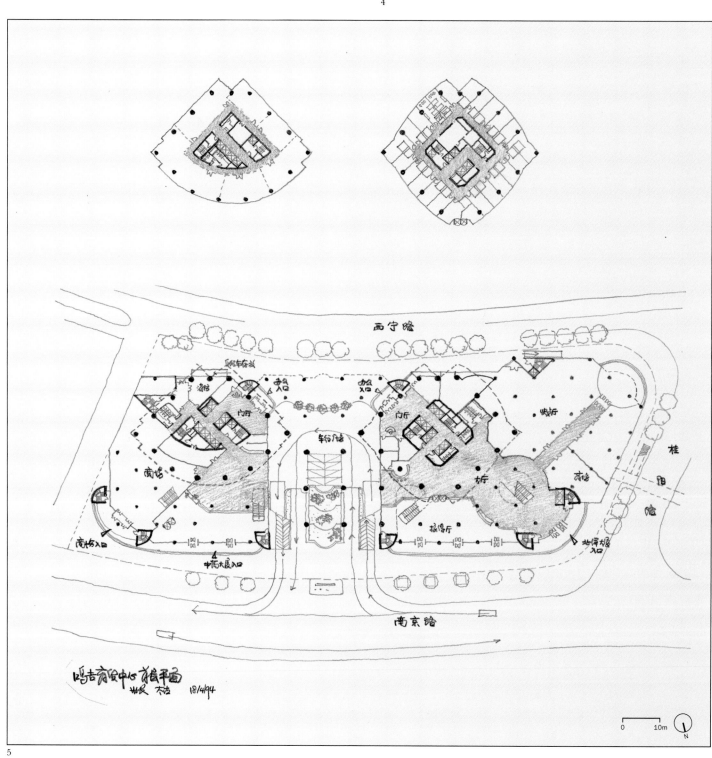

5

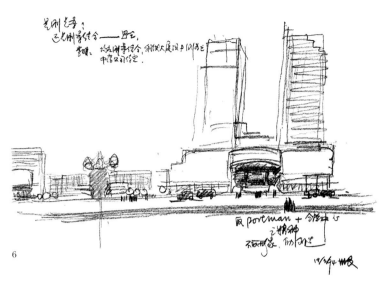

6

7

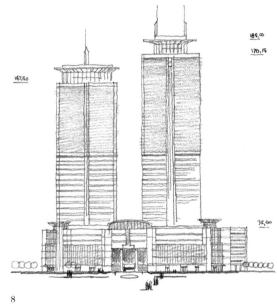

8

9

Great World Commercial Center

Schematic & preliminary design/Completion 1994/1999
Dalian, China
Dalian Great World Commercial Center Co. Ltd
Site area: 17,900 square meters
Total floor area: 190,000 square meters
Concrete
Stone, curtain wall, metal panel
In cooperation with Peddle Thorp Architects (Australia), Dalian
Architectural Design & Research Institute (China)
Winning international competition entry

This project is one of the landmarks of the city. It comprises three distinct towers: a 56-story office tower (214 meters high), a 36-story apartment building, and a 32-story hotel. The podium, which faces streets on three sides, is used for shops and recreation centers. A square—containing sculptures and green open space— is placed between the office and apartment buildings. The hotel, which faces northwest, enjoys a square of its own.

Designing the project as three independent towers over the podium allows the client to build and sell in phases and also simplifies the future management of the complex. Because of the cold climate in northern China, a curtain wall was not an efficient design option. The facade consists mainly of elongated windows with contrasting square and rounded shapes. The three towers are designed in different shapes and colors to create interesting outlines against the skyline and to give the complex a unique character.

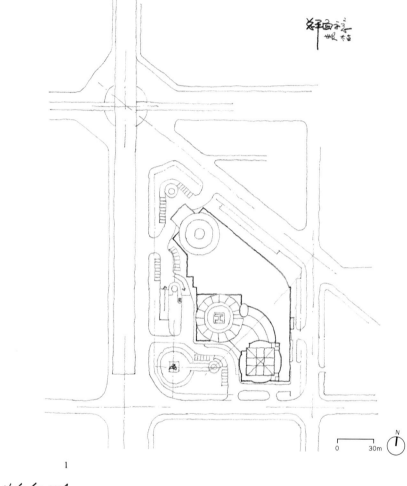

1

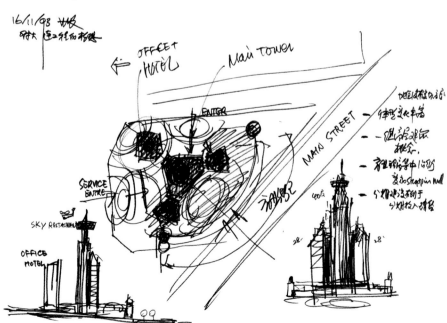

2

1 Site plan
2 First concept sketch
3 Model view showing three independent towers over the podium

136

3

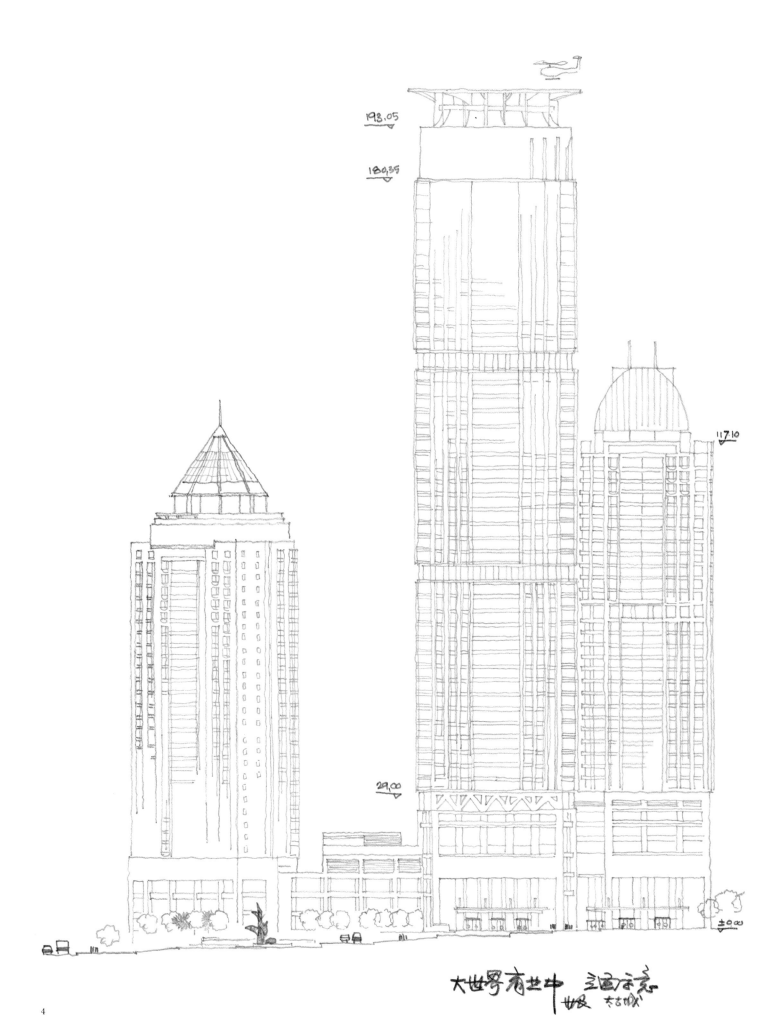

193.05

180.35

117.10

29.00

±0.00

大世界商业中心　三画室意
甘及　大古城

4 West elevation
5 Top of office and apartment towers
6 Ground level plan showing connection with the
   public square (left); office tower plan (above
   right); hotel tower plan (below right)
7 Model view showing the public square and entry
   to podium

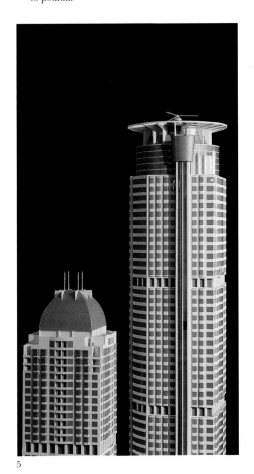

5

6

7

International Hotel and Commercial Plaza

Schematic design 1994–1995
Guangzhou, China
Fair Fund Industrial (Group) Ltd
Site area: 38,529 square meters
Total floor area: 380,000 square meters
Concrete
Curtain wall, metal panel, stone
Winning international competition entry

The site is located on the north side of the main thoroughfare in the center of Guangzhou, about 1.5 kilometers from the Guangzhou Railway Station. It faces a green open space and at its back is beautiful Baihun Mountain. The location thus enjoys both good access and a pleasant environment. However, the site is 4 to 5 meters higher than street level and is bisected by a rail line. Considering these factors, the general plan for this group of buildings is to arrange them on a terrace which follows the contours of the hill. The plan takes advantage of the sloping site by inserting a huge artificial slab, which forms an external square above, while concealing the railway line below. In addition, an oval-shaped public plaza is placed in front of the complex.

The complex comprises a 39-story apartment and hotel building and a 58-story office building. A multi-story atrium with a curved belt shape is located in the podium, which has some 50,000 square meters of floor space. The podium contains shops, a conference hall, exhibition space, recreation facilities, and a restaurant. The atrium is linked to the external plaza by an elliptically curved colonnade, creating a grand architectural space.

Parking facilities are located in the shopping area. Guangzhou is known as the "flower city," so six flower-shaped ornaments are placed on the top of the structure to add further character to the overall complex.

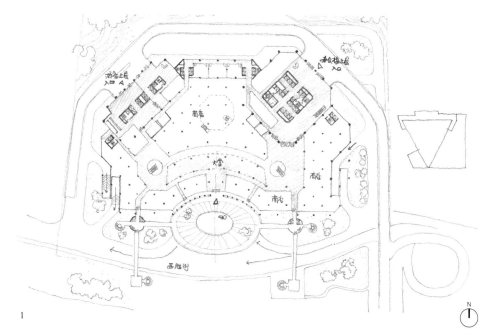

1

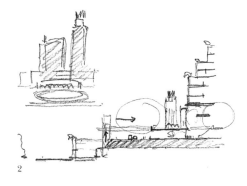

2

1 Ground level and site plan
2 Concept sketch
3 Model view from north
4 Model view from the park (south)

3

4

Chief Fine Building

Design/Completion 1994/1999
Nanjing, China
Nanjing Chief Fine Real Estate Co. Ltd
Site area: 3,720 square meters
Total floor area: 52,155 square meters
Concrete
Curtain wall, aluminum panel

The building is located on a limited site on the north side of the main thoroughfare in the commercial center of Nanjing. The side of the building adjacent to this thoroughfare comprises a five-story podium containing commercial space. The main entrance is located in a side street.

The complex contains apartments and offices for the accommodation of overseas businessmen. Over 230 luxury apartments are included, along with a restaurant, gymnasium, swimming pool, club, car parking, and other facilities tailored to the needs of these visitors.

The walls of the regular frame structure have smooth corners and exhibit diversity in design. Eight aluminum panels at the top of the building evoke an image of "a thousand sails."

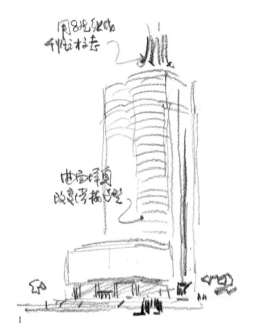

1

2

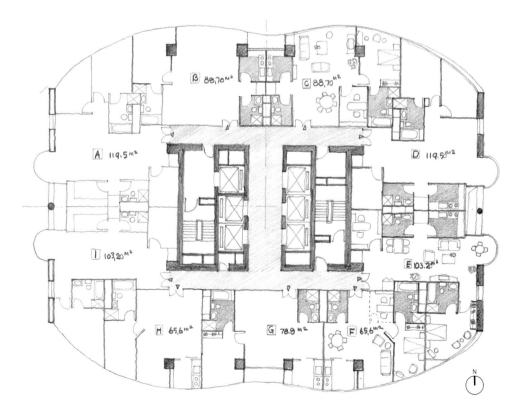

1   First concept sketch
2   Model view from main street (south)
3   Typical apartment level plan
4   Perspective view from south

3

142

4

Wango Plaza

Schematic & preliminary design 1994–1995
Guangzhou, China
Wango Group Company
Site area: 10,210 square meters
Total floor area: 119,700 square meters
Concrete
Stone, curtain wall, metal panel
Winning international competition entry

The site is at the center of Guangzhou's new downtown, on an axis with the Tianhe Stadium. An existing hotel and office building occupy the south and north corners of the square at the front of the site. In response to this context, twin saucer-shaped towers were designed. Together with the square and existing buildings, these towers form a cohesive whole with the stadium.

The south tower houses a luxury hotel, while the north tower is an office building. The five-story podium contains a restaurant, conference rooms, shops, and spaces for recreation and sport. From a common lobby, escalators and overhead passageways connect all levels to create a flowing and accessible space. In accordance with the client's request, a spherical restaurant is placed on the top of the main building. Orbiting satellite structures are located on the observation deck attached to the sphere.

The facades of the buildings use vertical shades and rounded windows to project an upright yet warm appearance.

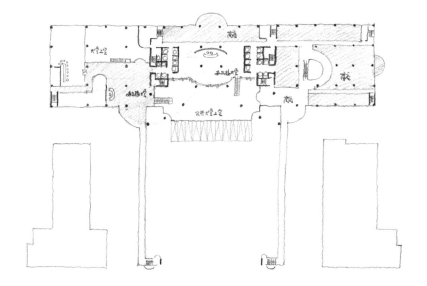

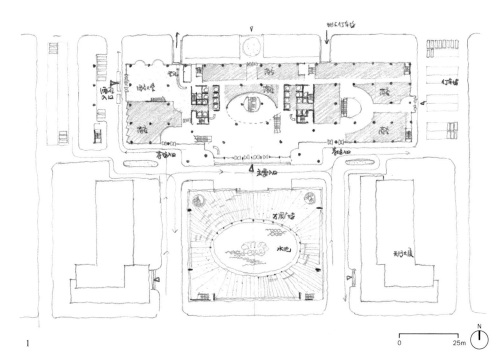

1   Site plan (below); podium plan (middle); hotel and office tower plans (above)
2   Concept sketch
3   Model elevation from east square
4   Model elevation from west
5   Aerial view of square

1

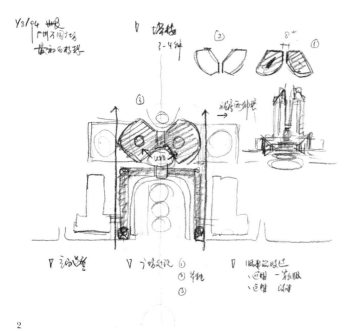

2

3

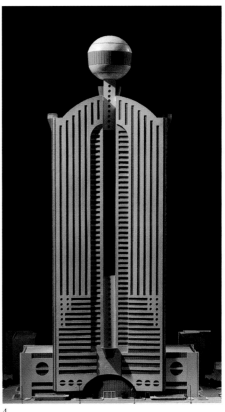

4

5

Seg Plaza

Design/Completion 1995/1999
Shenzhen, China
Seg Plaza Investment & Development Co. Ltd
Site area: 9,653 square meters
Total floor area: 157,953 square meters
Steel, concrete
Curtain wall, metal panel, stone
Winning competition entry

The site is in the center of downtown Shenzhen. The plaza provides exhibition space, offices, department stores, commercial information and recreation facilities, and a stock exchange. With a total height of 278 meters, the new building consists of 68 stories above ground, in the podium and tower, and a four-story underground car park. On completion, it will be a major landmark in the city of Shenzhen.

Because the site is at an intersection, it was not possible to place a square in front of it. Instead, the tower is placed at the northeast corner and the podium stretches along the street frontage.

A public square is placed in a three-story half-open space on the first floor level, leaving maximum floorspace for retail at street level. The half-open square provides easy access to the adjacent light rail system, as well as to elevated passageways, escalators, and stairs leading to the offices, shops, and car park. Provision is also made for future subway access. In this way, vehicles and pedestrians are safely separated.

The tower is octagonal in plan, with an overall column grid of 43.2 meters by 43.2 meters. Elevators, stairs, sanitary facilities, and other service functions are placed at the center. The structure is a tube of reinforced concrete and represents the tallest building of its type in the world. The facade is a gray glass curtain wall with gold-outlined aluminum panels, giving an appearance of noble simplicity.

The project has a Neo-Classical flavor, providing a unique architectural presence in Shenzhen. The glass curtain wall, belt windows, and colorful bands of the facade give the building a simple, clear, and upright aspect. On the top level, a club and bar, a helicopter pad, and satellite antennas add to the building's high-tech appearance.

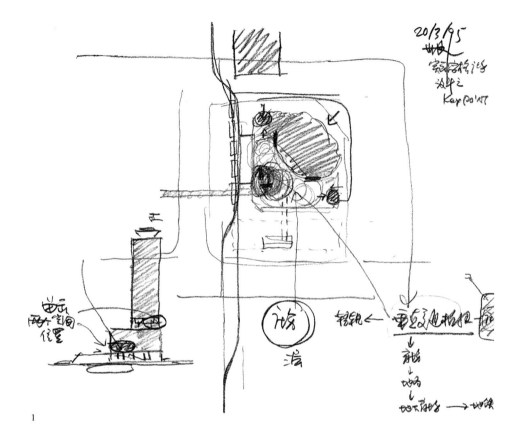

1

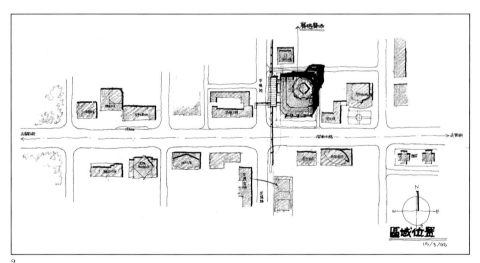

2

1   Initial concept sketch
2   Site plan
3   Study sketch of main street view
4   General view from west

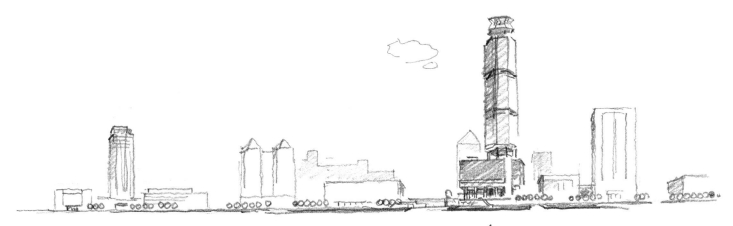

3

密檐广场占据
城市干道空间的控制性位置

4

5 Ground floor plan (below); first floor plan with
public open square (middle); tower
floor plan (top)

6 Tower view

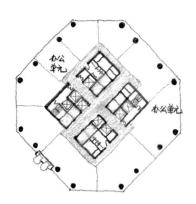

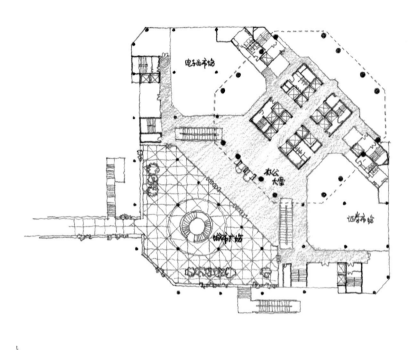

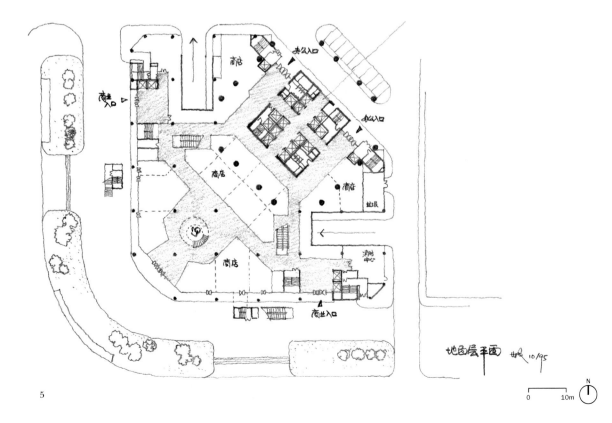

5

6

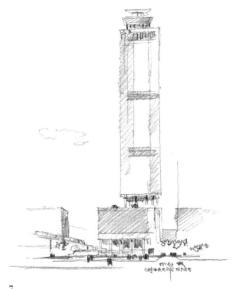

7

9

8

10

11

12

13

7   Elevation sketch
8   View from southwest
9   Tower top with helicopter platform
10   Public open square
11   View of the public open space
12   Interior of the main lobby
13   Interior of commercial space

Commercial Town, Futian

Design/Completion 1995/1999
Shenzhen, China
Shenzhen Lushan Garden Real Estate Development Co. Ltd,
Shenzhen Yimpeng Real Estate Co. Ltd
Site area: 11,769 square meters
Total floor area: 105,709 square meters
Reinforced concrete
Stone, tile, glass, curtain wall
Winning competition entry

This project is in the developing Futian District of Shenzhen, close to Shennanzhonglu Road, a main thoroughfare. The site is flat but is 2.5 meters to 3.5 meters lower than the surrounding roads. As a result, the vehicle entrance is elevated, and the lobby and public square are at the first floor level. The different functions within the complex have their own entrances, and vehicles and pedestrians are separated to ensure safe and easy access. The entrances to the office tower and shopping areas are located at the intersection in order to attract customers.

The four apartment buildings line up on the west and south sides of the site. The buildings are "butterfly-shaped" in plan, to maximize natural lighting and ventilation and to take full advantage of the views. The siting of the apartments around the periphery leaves the center of the site free for commercial space, underground car parks, and a roof garden.

The office tower is in the shape of a fan. Internal circulation is concentrated around a central structural hub, ensuring that the offices take maximum advantage of the views and natural lighting.

The latest commercial models were used as references for the project's commercial space. The complex provides all the necessary facilities to cater for the occupants of the offices and apartments, as well as services for the general public. The weatherproof four-story-high shopping mall provides rest, recreation, and exhibition areas in addition to shopping space. A transfer plate structure is used to create a space which is both large and versatile.

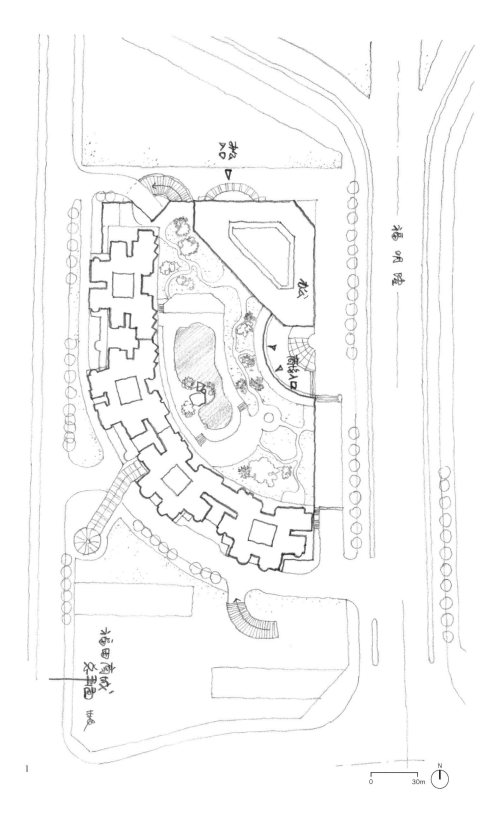

1

0   30m

1   Master plan
2   Concept study sketch
3   Street view from east

152

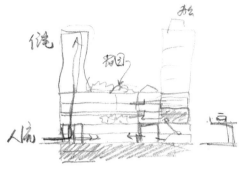

2

3

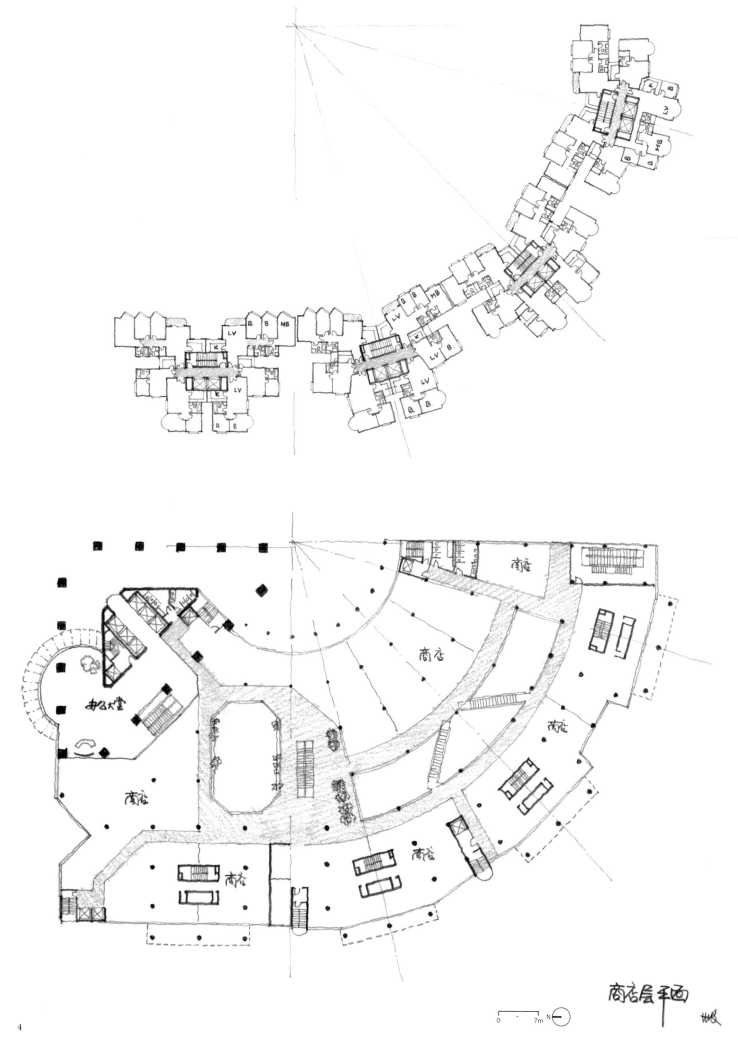

商店层平面

0 · 7m N

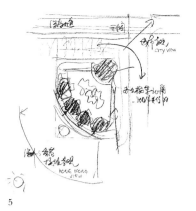

5

6

7

8

7   View of apartment buildings from above
8   Aerial view: between the office tower and the apartment building is a podium
    accommodating a large roof garden and a swimming pool

Daxin Building

Schematic design/Completion 1997/2000
Chongqing, China
Daxin Housing Development Ltd
Site area: 10,100 square meters
Total floor area: 101,250 square meters
Concrete
Stone, curtain wall, metal panel
In cooperation with The China Southwest Architectural
Design & Research Institute

This is a re-design project which involves integrating the existing disordered and massive development into a single entity. In order to achieve this, a multi-function tower and a purpose-designed podium were created after a detailed environmental study.

Passageways and columns are added to the three-story podium along the main thoroughfare to bring a sense of connectedness to the disjointed built environment and to introduce an element of style. A playground is located at the top of the podium, along with the original five-story primary school structure. This playground has easy access to the neighboring middle school, improving the overall school layout.

On the east side of the project, a small square is designed as the entrance to the podium and to the complex itself. The tower, which houses hotels and offices, is located to the west, facing the main intersection. This provides maximum accessibility to the podium from all directions, benefiting the retail tenants.

A passageway connecting the eastern and western sides of the complex is located in the center of the podium, facilitating access to all the shops. Different facade treatments for the upper and lower sections of the tower distinguish the hotel rooms from the offices. The roof gardens, placed on different levels, provide a green environment in this humid and crowded city, and constitute one of the highlights of the project.

1

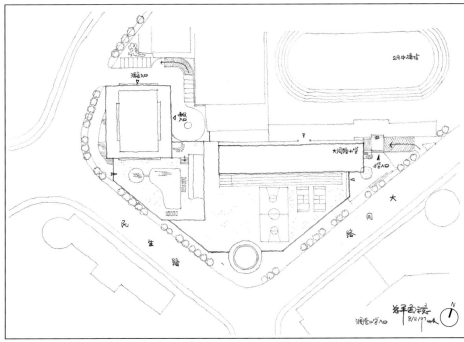

1 Sketch
2 Site plan
3 Perspective showing general view from the street

2

3

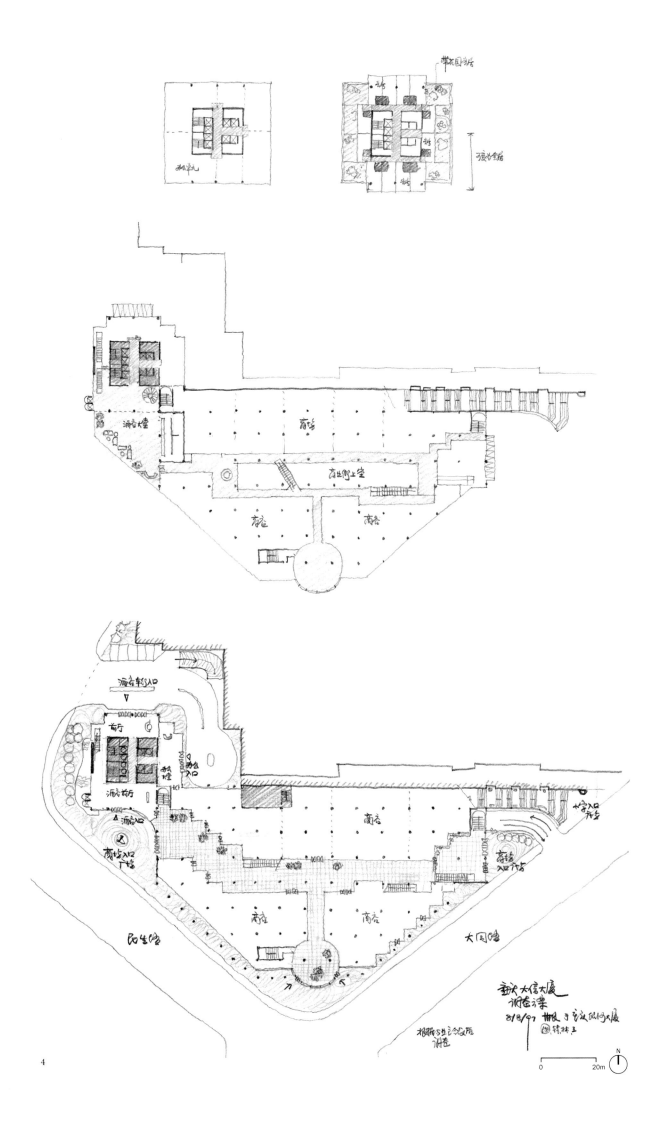

4 Ground floor plan (below); second floor plan (middle);
 office/hotel floor plan (above)
5 General view showing the connection between the
 tower, the primary school building, and playground
 located in the podium

5

Qiaoguang Plaza

Schematic design 1997
Shenzhen, China
New Century Industrial (Holdings) Ltd
Site area: 12,841 square meters
Total floor area: 142,000 square meters
Reinforced concrete
Stone, glass, metal panel
Joint venture with China Aeronautical Project & Design Institute

This project was initially intended to be a general complex of shops and apartments. However, once construction had begun and the basement had been completed, the client decided to change the design to respond to changes in the real estate market. The seven-story podium over the main street was subsequently redesigned to accommodate a commercial center and a banking hall. On the top floor of the podium, a multi-function hall, conference rooms, ballrooms, bars, a billiards room, and other recreation facilities were incorporated. The two multi-story towers were reassigned to house bank offices and a hotel.

On the ground floor, separate entrances were designed facing the main street. A helicopter pad was included on the top of the hotel tower for fire-fighting purposes. The facade is composed of huge columns and vertical lines which run the full height of the towers, together with Western-style colored glass and stone. While they share an identical color and material palette, the two towers are quite different in appearance.

1 Concept sketch
2 Main street view of model

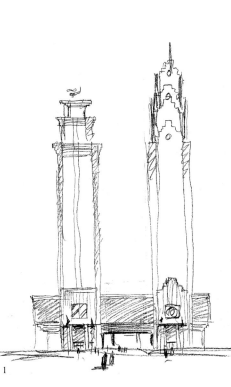

1

2

Pingan Plaza

Schematic & preliminary design/Completion 1997/2000
Shanghai, China
China Ping An Trust & Investment Company
Site area: 8,000 square meters
Total floor area: 75,500 square meters
Reinforced concrete
Stone, glass
In cooperation with East China Architectural Design & Research Institute

The site, on the well-known Huaihaixilu Road, at the boundary between the commercial and cultural districts of Shanghai, formerly housed an education institute. This is replaced by an insurance office building, an educational classroom structure, and a podium housing commercial facilities.

The site's irregular shape, bounded by streets on all three sides, complicated the process of designing a building which encompassed these three quite different functions. After examining many options, the preferred solution was to build two towers with a connecting commercial podium. The office tower faces the main street, while the smaller educational building is assigned a quiet location which provides access both to the street and to existing teaching facilities. The commercial podium is utilized as a natural connection between the two towers. It also provides a clear distinction between client identities.

The architectural language of the building facades depicts the general character of each client but also expresses their individual styles. At the same time, a relationship to the general built environment is established.

1 Concept sketch
2 Street view from Huaihai Road

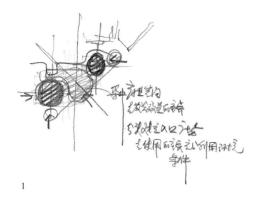

1

2

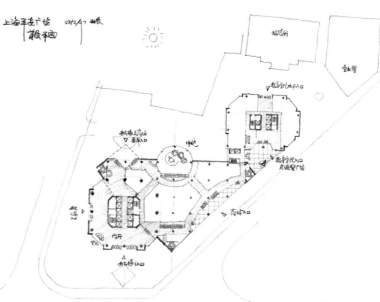

4

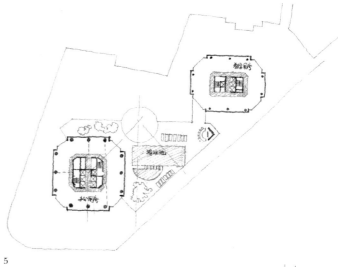

5

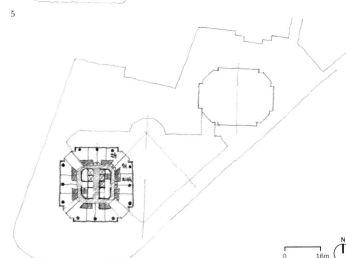

6

3 Aerial view of model from the north, showing the compatible design treatment of the insurance office building (high-rise) and the educational classroom structure (low-rise)

4 Ground level plan

5 Mid-rise level office plan

6 High-rise level apartment plan

7 Elevation sketches

N

0   16m

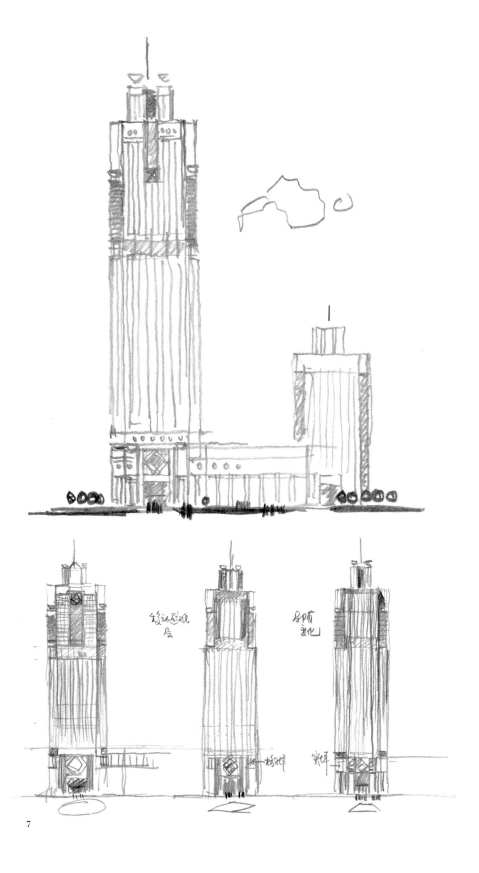

7

OFFICE
BUILDINGS

Shenzhen Financial Center

Schematic & preliminary design/Completion 1983/1986
Shenzhen, China
Construction Administration of Shenzhen Municipal Government
Site area: 48,480 square meters
Total floor area: 128,900 square meters
Concrete
Tile, glass, stone
In cooperation with Shenzhen Project & Research Institute of NMIC (China)

This project involves three towers which house two major independent banks and a luxury hotel. It is situated in the financial and commercial area of Shenzhen, at the intersection of two main thoroughfares.

In order to integrate the three towers into a single entity, they are placed at an angle of 120 degrees to each other around a common central square, suggesting a spirit of unity. The podium is organized in terraces between the towers, creating a sense of verticality, as with a statue. The project utilizes the concept of multi-directional composition, so the banks and the hotel have their own entrances leading onto the square. The three towers coexist at the center of the site. Around the buildings on all sides, wide green spaces are located for the enjoyment of the public.

In the podium, a triangular column grid is used. Each side is 7.5 meters long, emphasizing the multi-directional composition of the general plan. The three towers are rectangular in plan, and employ a column grid that is suitable for both office and hotel functions.

The podium organizes pedestrian traffic within and beyond the site, connecting with an overpass that leads to the city. The second level of the podium provides an ideal pedestrian environment.

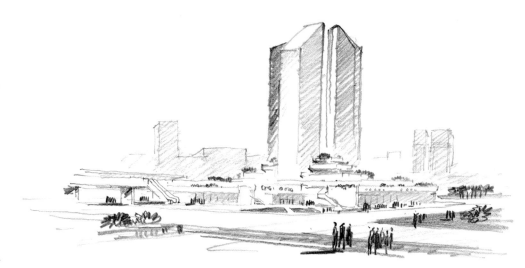

1

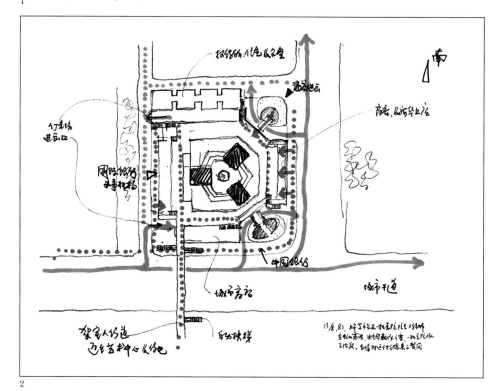

2

1 Concept sketch
2 Sketch of master plan
3 General view from main street

3

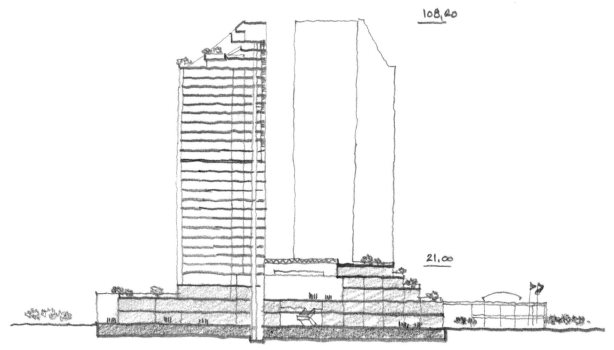

4

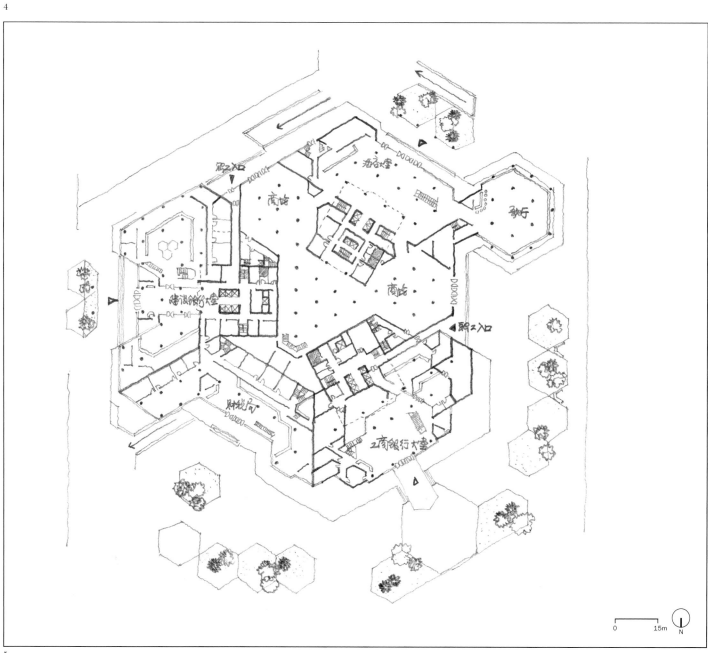

酒店大堂

商店

银行

建设银行大堂

商店

工商银行大堂

财税局

0 15m

N

5

4 Section
5 Ground level plan
6 Concept sketches
7 View from east
8 View from lake of City park

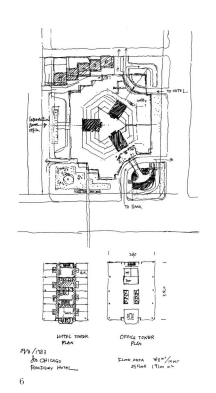

6

7

8

9

10

11

12

9&10   Hotel lobby
11&12 Bank chamber for Shenzhen Industrial & Commercial Bank of China
13   Hotel restaurant
14&15 Bank chamber for Shenzhen China Construction Bank

13

14

15

Office Building, Gintian

Design/Completion 1991/1994
Shenzhen, China
Shenzhen Gintian Real Estate Development Co.
Site area: 1,695 square meters
Total floor area: 18,800 square meters
Concrete
Curtain wall, stone

The building occupies a tight site at an intersection on the main road in the city, close to other apartment buildings. It contains a bank, offices, apartments, meeting rooms, recreation spaces, and gymnasiums. The main design problems involved satisfying fire-fighting regulations and adapting to the busy traffic around the site. The plan is composed of two quarter circles. This shape maintains good visibility for vehicular traffic at the intersection, while also permitting some public open space to be included in front of the building. In addition, the ground floor is raised and the lobby set back to provide a feeling of spaciousness in the confined city environment.

Because of regulations governing the site, each floor is limited to 700 square meters. The structural system occupies a minimal amount of space. Apart from the structural columns for the main traffic access, the design uses a limited number of columns to provide flexibility in the use of the available space.

The curved facade, with its golden glass curtain wall, adds character to the busy commercial district of the city.

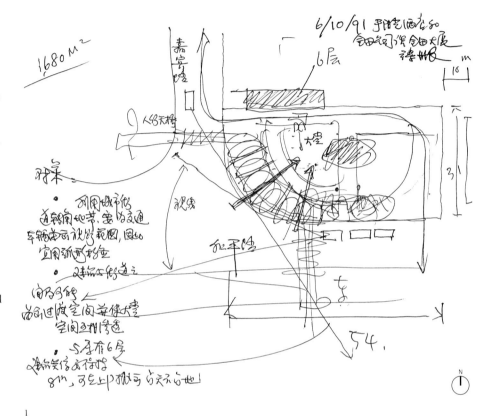

1

2

3

1 Initial study sketch
2 View from north
3 Concept sketch
4 Gold glass curtain wall facade

174

4

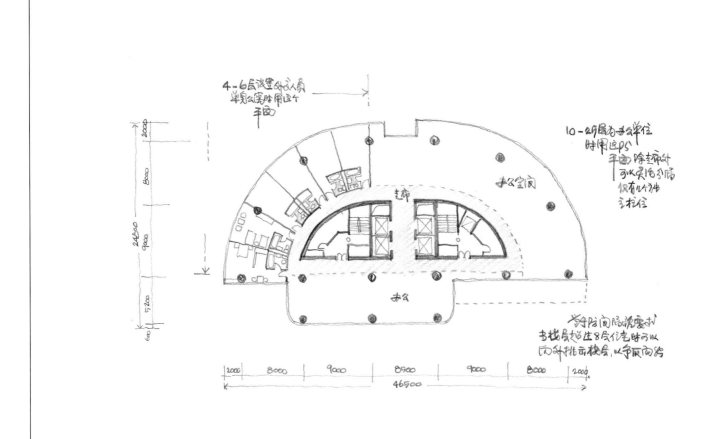

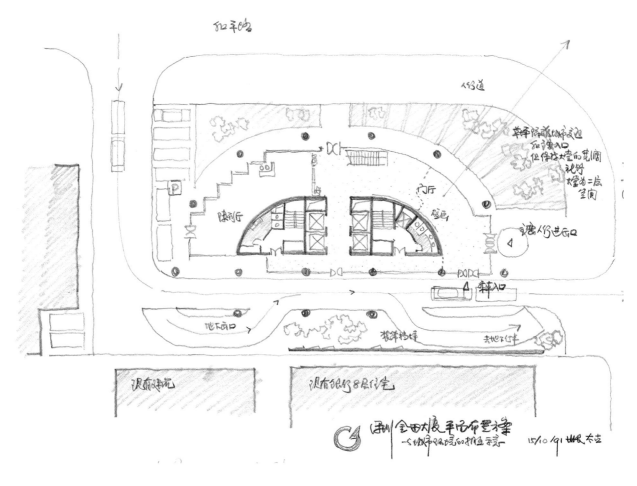

6

7

8

5 Tower level plan (above) and
   ground level plan (below)
6 Main entrance
7 Lobby view
8 Elevator lobby

Development Bank Building, Shenzhen

Design/Completion 1992/1996
Shenzhen, China
Shenzhen Development Bank Ltd
Site area: 99,363 square meters
Total floor area: 56,320 square meters
Concrete
Curtain wall, stone
Schematic design in cooperation with Peddle Thorp Architects (Australia)
Winning competition entry

The site is right at the center of the city, to the south of the main thoroughfare. It is next to the Shenzhen Financial Center building, and at the starting point of a series of high-rise buildings. These factors, together with the client's brief, determined that a modern building with a unique outlook was required.

Within the limits of the site, a girdle column grid plan is applied, and a pyramid-like terrace ascends into the sky. This contrasts dramatically with the adjacent bank building, establishing the project's unique character.

The facade is a simple composition of a granite skirt, glass curtain wall, and aluminum panels. An upward-tilting stainless steel structure is used to express the semantics of strength, power, and mechanics, and also to add a 21st century high-technology aesthetic.

The office lobby and the banking chamber are placed side by side. The five-story-high banking chamber hall is the most magnificent space of its kind in the city, and has proven to be very popular for its sense of openness. To one side of the staircases, glazed interior gardens at different levels provide public space for the offices. These gardens transform the traditional closed office design into a modern, comfortable, and intelligent work space incorporating the natural environment.

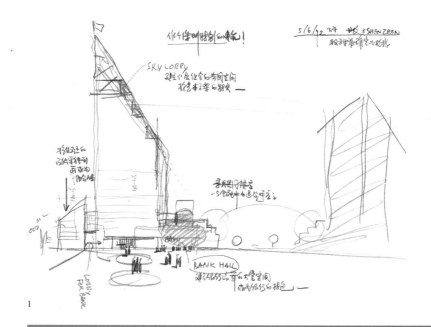

1

2

3

1 Concept sketch
2 Site plan sketch
3 View of the city's main thoroughfare from west
4 View of building facade from north

5

6

7

8

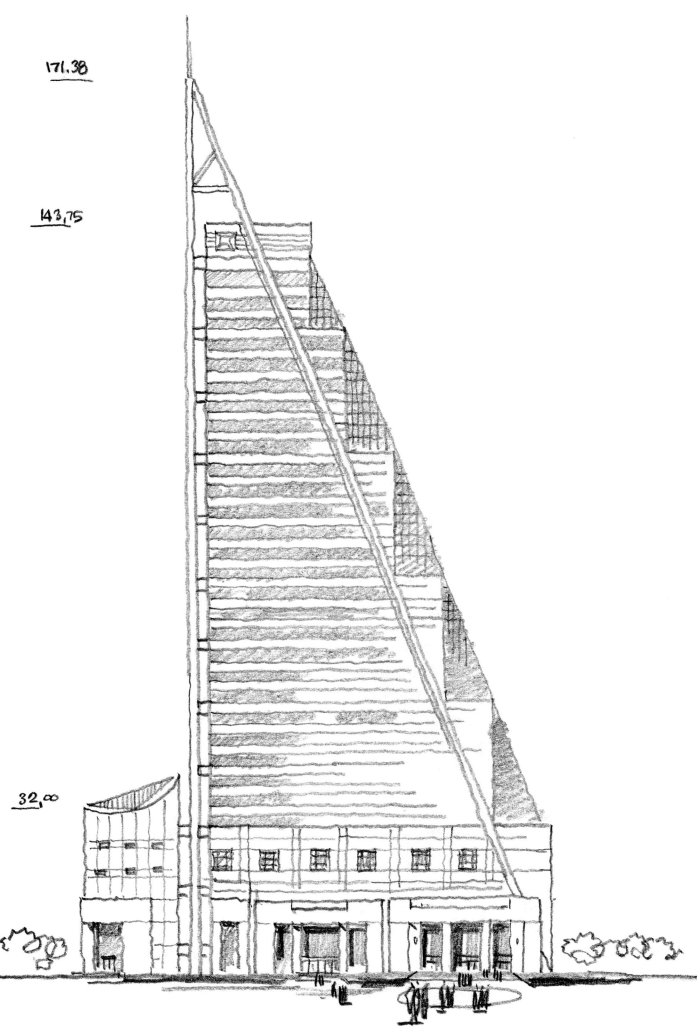

171.38

143,75

32,00

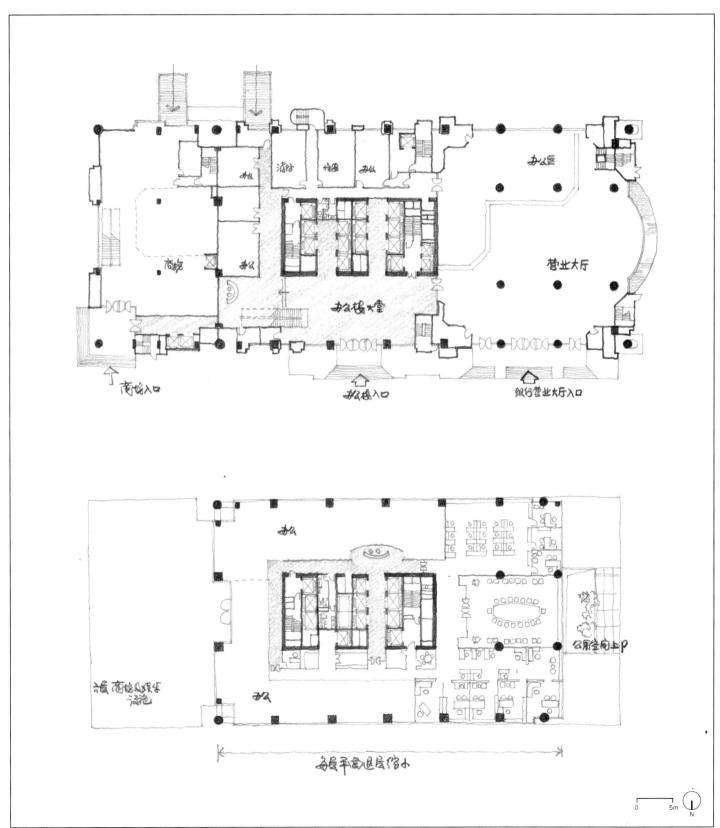

10

12

13

14

12 View up inside the bank chamber
13 Bank chamber interior
14 West door of bank chamber
15 Office reception space
16 Office interior

15

16

Foreign Trade Center Building

Schematic & preliminary design 1988
Shenzhen, China
Shenzhen Sez Foreign Trade (Group) Corp.
Site area: 4,961 square meters
Total floor area: 42,000 square meters
Concrete
Stone, glass, tile

This project is in a poorly organized part of the city. A hexagonal shape is used to allow the building to blend into and enhance the complex built environment.

The ground floor is raised and the main building is set back from the street to provide space for a lawn and ponds. This arrangement eases the crowded pedestrian and vehicle circulation and reduces the noise level. It also beautifies the environment. The tower is based on a triangular column grid, while the podium is formed by two combined hexagons. Glass-enclosed fire stairs are placed on the outside of the building to save space and add a sense of verticality to the building. The shining sphere on the top of the structure is the hallmark of this project.

1 Model view from north
2 Typical mid-rise floor plan (above) and ground level plan (below)
3 View of model from main street

1

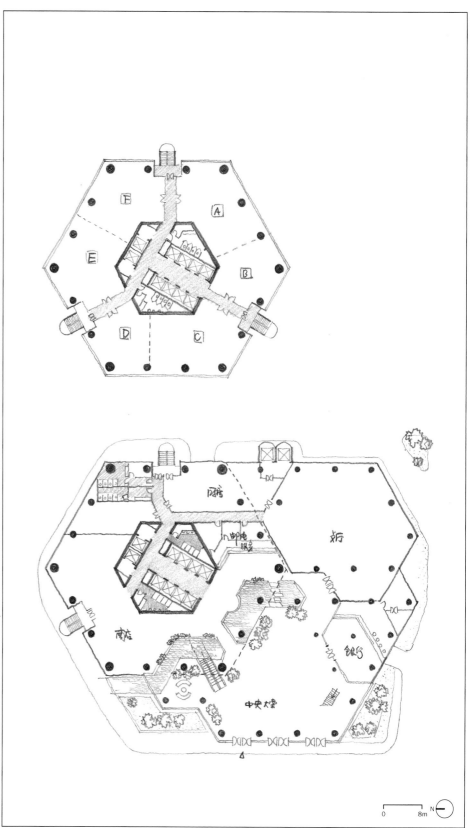

2

186

3

Fenglong Center

Competition 1995
Shenzhen, China
Shenzhen Fenglong Enterprise Development Co. Ltd
Site area: 14,413 square meters
Total floor area: 176,415 square meters
Concrete
Curtain wall, metal panel

The project is a high-rise complex which includes an office building, a department store, and parking for 500 vehicles. The site is to the southwest of the intersection of two main roads. The plan specifies a subway with two entrances. One entrance will be in the building itself, with the second entrance located off the square, facilitating pedestrian access.

Vehicle access to the building is limited by the site. Accordingly, a public parking lot and a small square are placed to the west to facilitate both vehicle and pedestrian access.

The seven-story podium on the east is designed for commercial use. The podium is designed so that its levels correspond with those of the nearby urban transportation system and also to provide additional circulation space.

The dominant elements of the facade are a simple blue glass curtain wall combined with white vertical lines, creating a unique modern appearance.

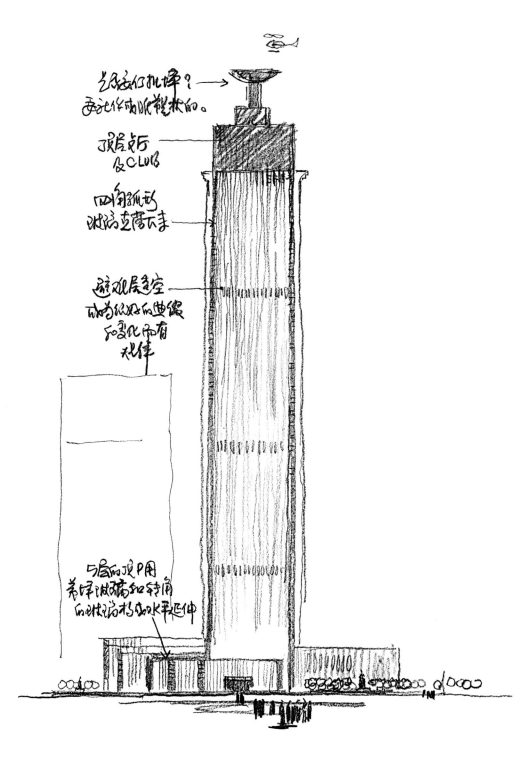

1 Elevation sketch
2 Overall view of model from north

1

188

2

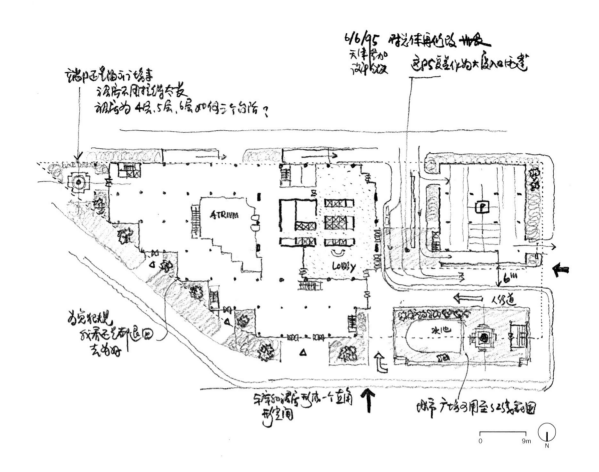

ATRIVM

LOBBY

6m

人行道

水池

0   9m   N

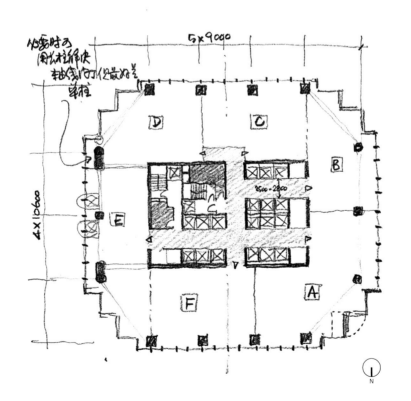

5×9000

4×10600

D   C

B

E

F   A

N

3 Ground floor plan (above) and typical
  office floor plan (below)
4 East view showing the main city street
5 Aerial view of podium

Bocom Finance Tower

Competition 1996
Shanghai, China
Shanghai Bocom Finance Tower Co. Ltd
Site area: 9,975 square meters
Total floor area: 100,000 square meters
Concrete
Stone, glass, curtain wall

The site of this bank building is in the downtown area of the Lujiazhui trading district of Shanghai. It has green space to the front and the Huangpu River to the rear. The busiest section of Shanghai is located across the river, so this site enjoys a good environment and varied views.

The project comprises a single diamond-shaped tower and a half-diamond-shaped podium. The simple appearance of the structure blends with the environment. The four-story-high banking hall with its natural lighting at the top gives the building a unique character. The multi-function hall at the top of the tower is supported on glass-like columns which run the full height of the building, giving it the appearance of a flying object during the day. At night it is illuminated to become a grand beacon.

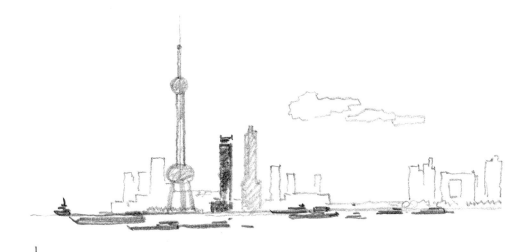

1

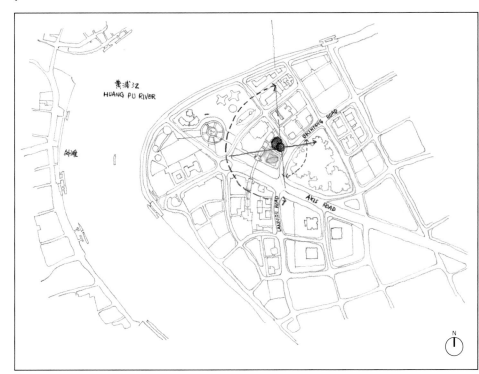

2

1 Study sketch of tower form
2 Site and location plan
3 Overall view of model

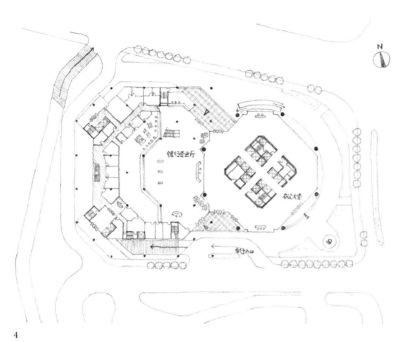

4

5

7

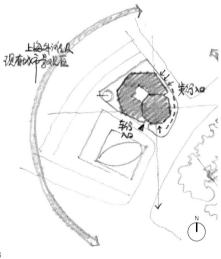

8

6

Communication Bank Building, Suzhou Branch

Competition 1996
Suzhou, China
Communication Bank, Suzhou Branch
Site area: 7,000 square meters
Total floor area: 29,980 square meters
Concrete
Stone, glass, metal panel

The project site is at the intersection of two main streets in the new administration district of the city. The main tower rises directly from ground level, facing the main street, to leave space for an open pedestrian forecourt. The podium is located to the rear of the building, over the vehicle entrance. A spacious hall is enclosed by a curved wall, forming a link with the environment.

The form of the main tower recalls the layers of a Chinese pagoda, making a symbolic connection with the famous ancient pagoda of Suzhou.

1

1   Second level plan
2   Street level view from southeast
3   View of model from north
4   Aerial view of model showing the building facing two main streets

2

3

Agricultural Bank, Shandong

Schematic & preliminary design/Completion 1996/1999
Jinan, China
Construction Administration of Shandong Agriculture Bank
Site area: 15,600 square meters
Total floor area: 81,300 square meters
Concrete
Stone, curtain wall, metal panel
In cooperation with Zhongian Architectural Design Institute of Jinan (China)
Winning competition entry

The project faces a Y-shaped junction of three main roads. Applying sound urban design principles, the axis of the building is aligned with the axis of symmetry of the three roads, and a pedestrian court is placed in front of the building. The podium is constructed on an 8.5 meter by 8.5 meter column grid, also in alignment with the direction of the roads.

The use of tall columns to form a portico establishes a grand rhythm around the base of the building. The tall tower, with its clear geometric shape, has become one of the landmarks of the city. The link between the court and the main building is the 18-meter-high lobby, which organizes the pedestrian circulation to the office building, the bank, and the conference hall.

The facade is formed using the contrasting materials of a glass curtain wall, and granite and aluminum panels. This, combined with the harmonious color palette, indicates the strength of the financial building. The top of the tower, quite characteristically, shines day and night.

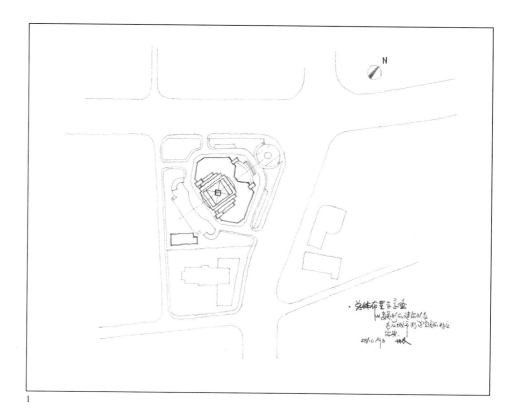

1

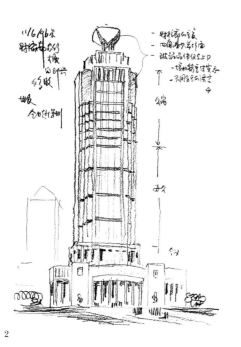

2

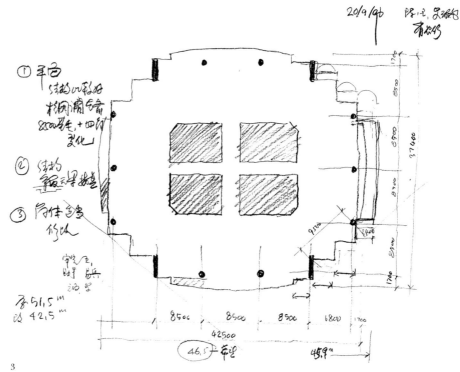

3

1   Site plan
2   Concept sketch
3   Study sketch of tower plan
4   Perspective showing the main (north) elevation

4

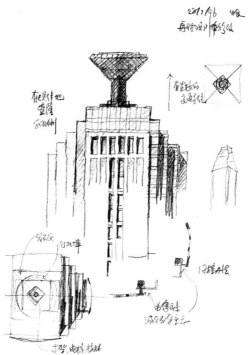

5 Model view from east
6 Study sketch of top of building
7 Ground level plan
8 Elevation sketch

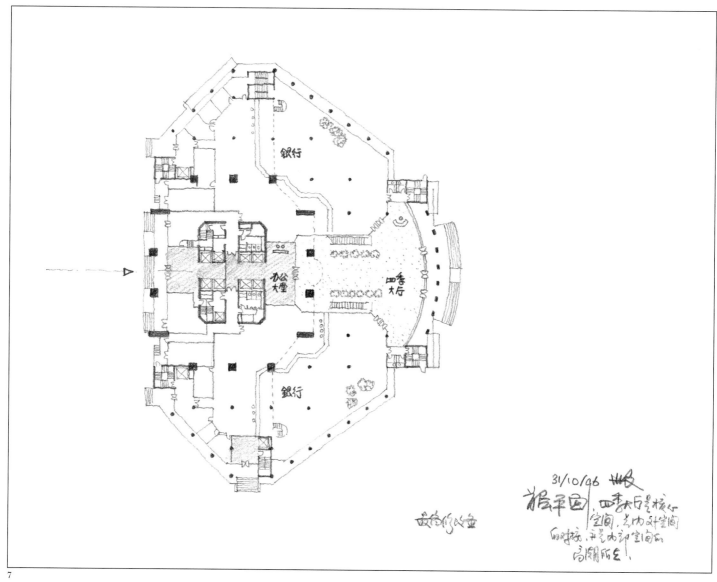

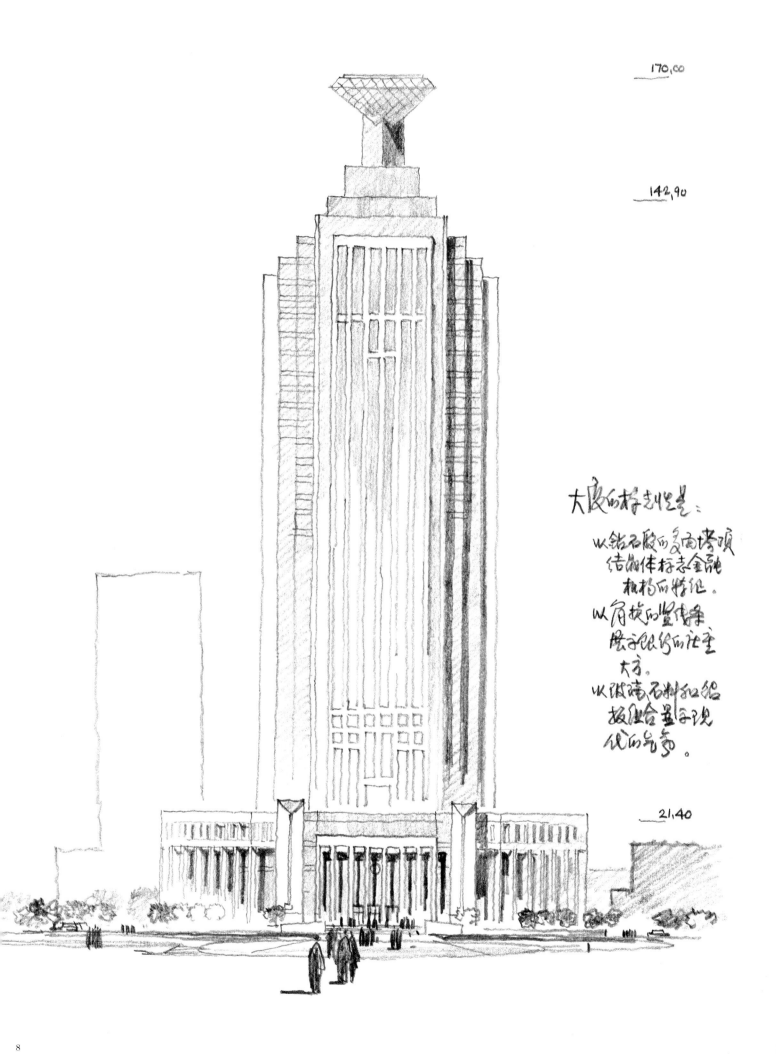

170,00

142,90

大度的构思是：

以钻石般的多面塔顶
结构体标志金融
机构的特征。

以肩挺的壁传承
感子银行的沉重
大方。

以玻璃,石料和铝
板组合显示现
代的气息。

21,40

8

Huanqing Building

Competition 1997
Shenzhen, China
Shenzhen Mercantile Exchange Co. Ltd
Site area: 7,890 square meters
Total floor area: 91,800 square meters
Concrete and steel
Curtain wall, stone, metal panel

This project involves the design of a building for stock exchange and futures trading activities. It comprises a trading hall, offices, shops, clubs, and other associated functions. The site faces the main city thoroughfare and also green space, so it enjoys a prominent location and a beautiful view. In order to avoid interference with the apartment building located in the east of the site, the main building is placed towards the thoroughfare, and the stock exchange trading hall is placed between the tower and the apartment building.

Design 1

This design consists of two towers of 177 meters, positioned at an angle of 45 degrees. At the lower part of the towers, a seven-story-high opening connects the trading hall to the main road and the green space. This is a metal structure in the form of a crystal. The glass curtain walls, metal panels, and glass caps are designed to reflect the building's financial function.

Design 2

This alternative design applies if the height of the building is limited to 100 meters. Here, the tower and podium blend into one, and the internal hall faces the main thoroughfare and the green space, providing a view of downtown Shenzhen.

The trading hall is placed at the top of the tower, accessed by externally positioned elevators. Clubs and offices are located in different layers, one on top of the other. The layers are lower at the front and higher at the back, forming three hanging gardens at different levels. These gardens will provide ventilation and shade to the building during the hot southern summer.

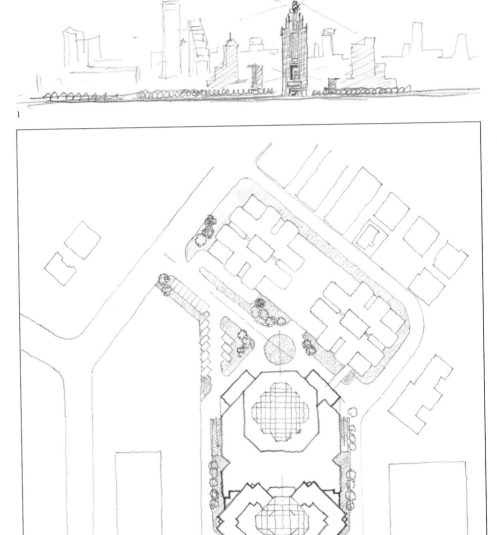

1

福 田 南 路

N

2

1   Initial concept sketch
2   Sketch of master plan
3   Perspective from west (Design 1)

3

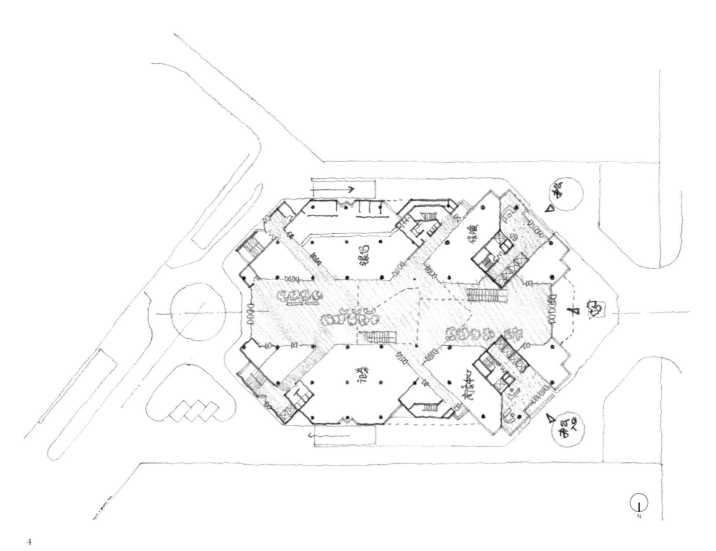

4

5

6

7

8 Concept sketch (Design 2)
9 Model view from north (Design 2)
10 Perspective from west (Design 2)
11 Model view from west (Design 2)

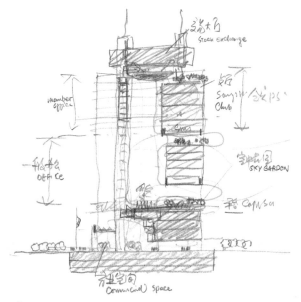

8

9

10

China Construction Corporation Complex, Chongqing

Design/Completion 1996/1999
Chongqing, China
China Building Equipment & Materials Corp. Ltd
Site area: 8,000 square meters
Total floor area: 77,040 square meters
Concrete
Curtain wall, metal panel, stone
In cooperation with Chongqing Iron & Steel Designing Institute

Chongqing lies at the confluence of the famous Yangtze and Jialing Rivers. The entire city is built upon hills. The project is located on a site from which the two rivers can be seen. When completed, the building will form a city landmark.

Two main factors influenced the design: the limited site area, and the requirement to provide a sports ground for the existing middle school as part of the complex. The resulting design concept involves making maximum use of the "sky" space while minimizing the footprint on the ground. The retail podium is located at a bend of the road, and a playground and student running tracks are placed on its roof.

The local architectural language of houses placed on stilts has been adopted for the structure. Eight main columns support the building, and the office floors stretch out in an elongated fashion. Three hanging gardens have been designed. All have a view of both rivers, providing comfortable, cool, and quiet places for people to rest in Chongqing's hot weather. These elements augment the local flavor of the building. In addition, four crystal-shaped structures are located on the top of the building. On foggy days, and at night, these emit a colorful light, creating a spiritual effect for the city residents.

1

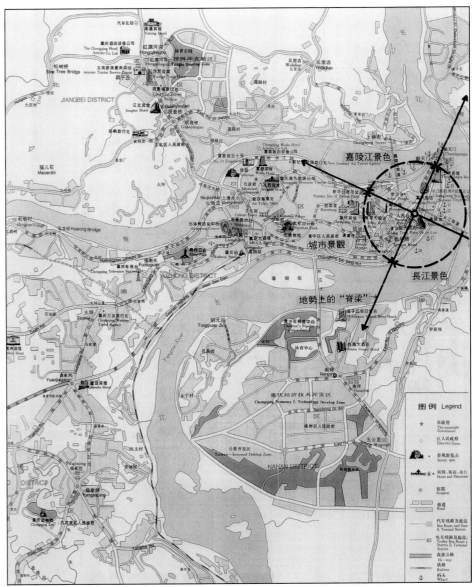

1   Initial concept sketch showing view from river
2   Location map
3   Aerial view of model from south corner

2

3

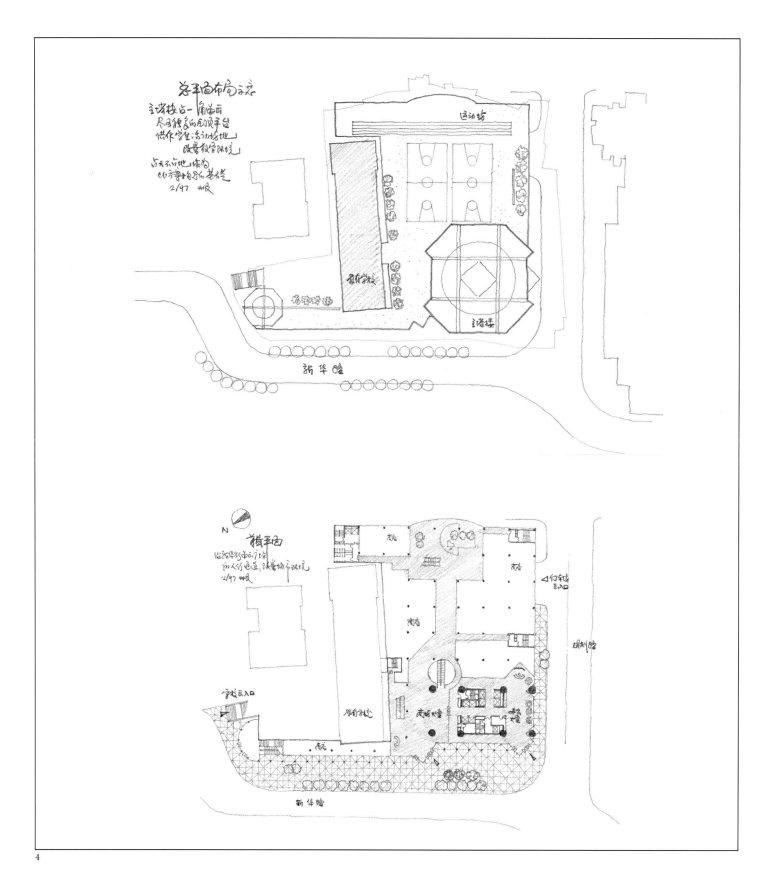

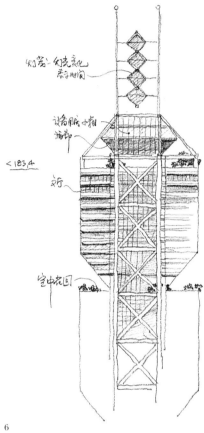

6

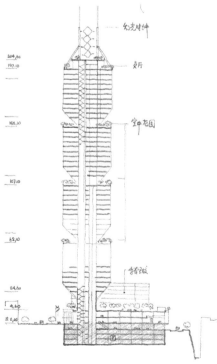

7

4 Master plan (above) and ground level plan (below)
5 Street elevation of model
6 Detailed sketch of top of tower
7 Sketch of section

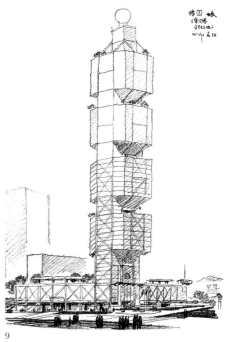

8   Night view showing the colored lights which act
     as beacons for boats on the two rivers
9   Elevation study sketch
10   Interior view of lobby
11   Perspective view from southwest

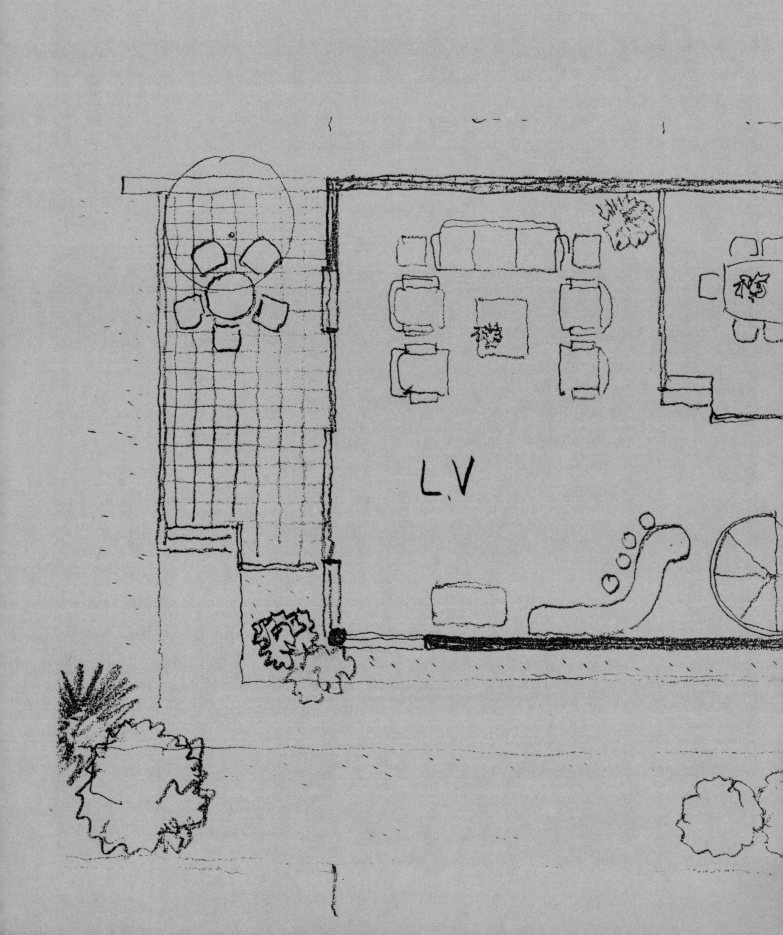

LV

RESIDENTIAL BUILDINGS

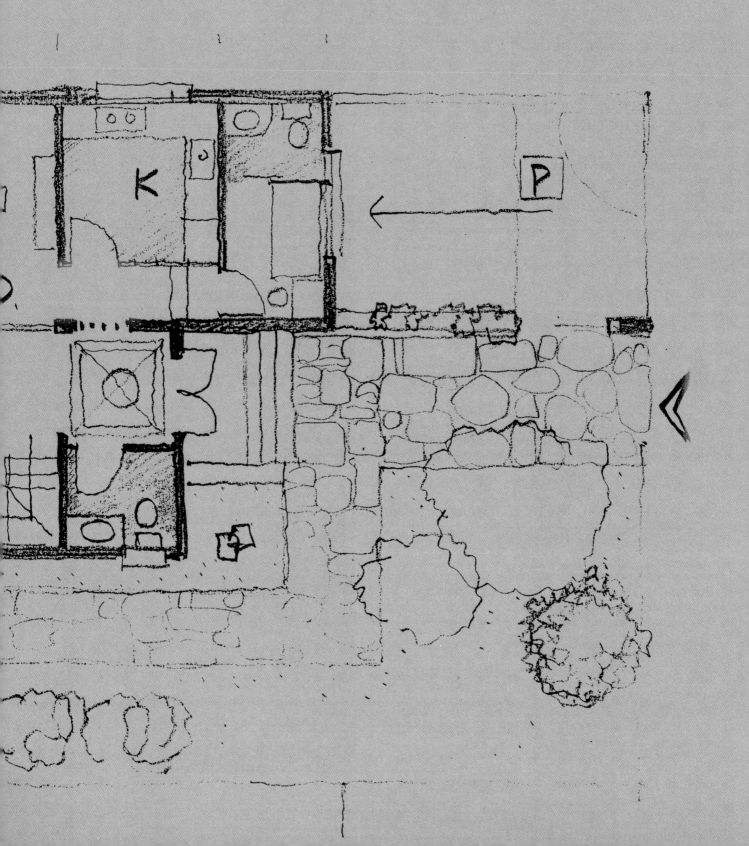

Commercial and Apartment Building, Caiwuwei

Design/Completion 1993/1999
Shenzhen, China
Shenzhen Caiwuwei Development Co. Ltd
Site area: 4,765 square meters
Total floor area: 54,267 square meters
Concrete
Stone, glass, tile

This project forms a triangle with the Financial Center and the Development Bank. To emphasize this triangular form, the project is designed as two diamond-shaped towers combined in a V shape. The podium is the same height as the Financial Center, and the top of the building takes the form of a terrace, which harmonizes with the finance center and the bank.

The apartments come in two main sizes of 40 square meters and 90 square meters, to suit the different needs of the residents. The facade combines a transparent glass curtain wall and a solid wall in proportions which change with the elevation. The simple architectural language applied to these elevations allows the building to blend into its environment.

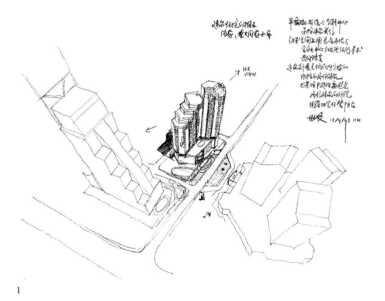

1

1 Study sketch showing the relationship with nearby buildings
2 Main view from northwest

2

216

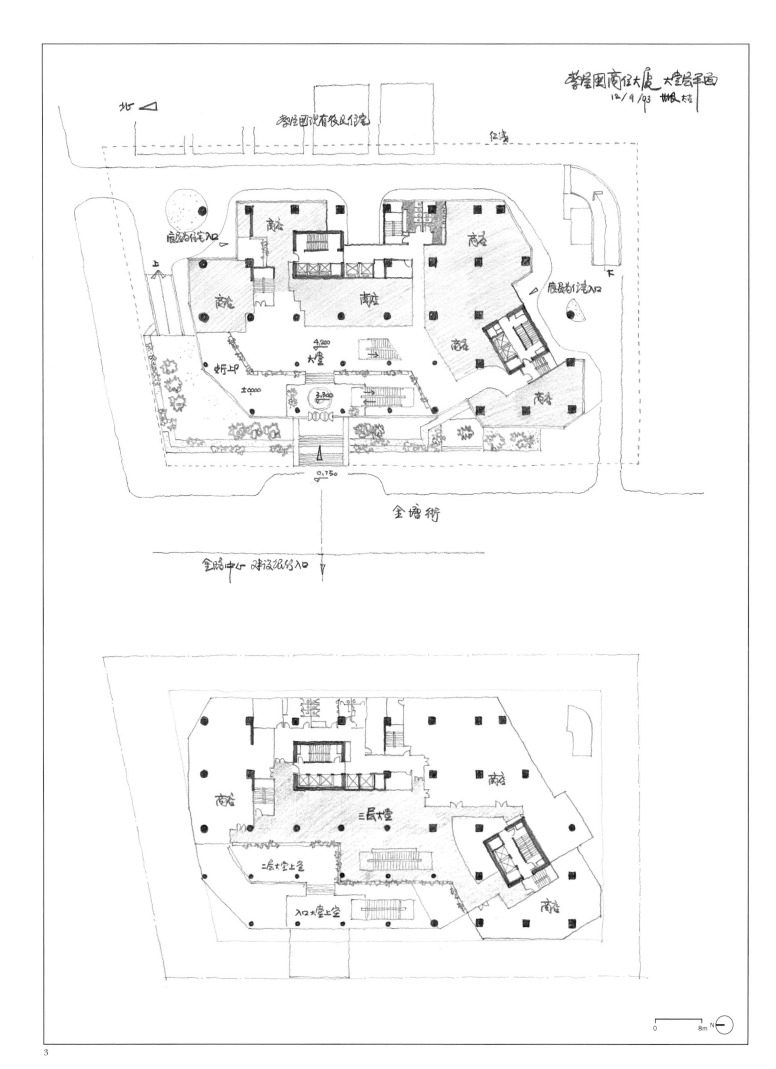

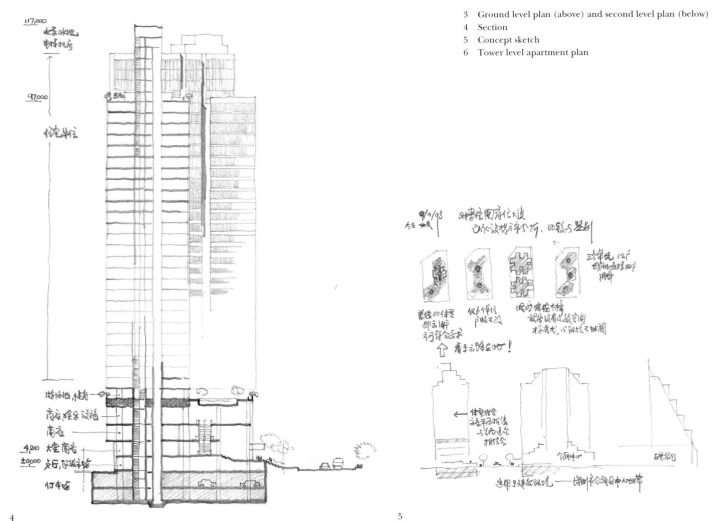

4

5

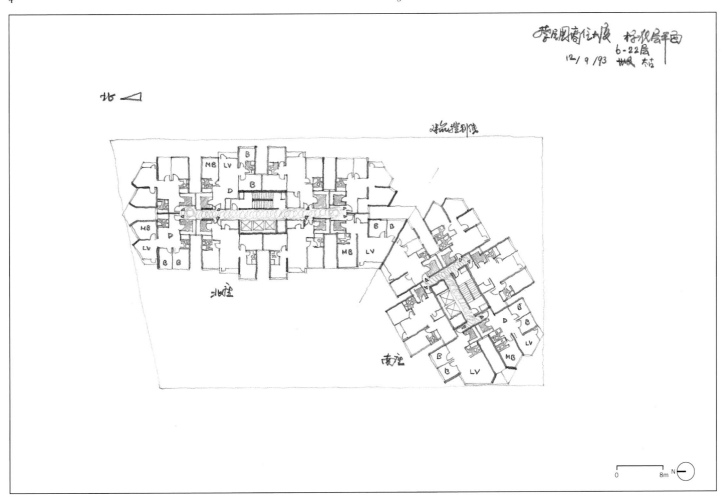

6

Rose Garden

Schematic design/Completion 1997/2000
Shenzhen, China
Shenzhen Maigaol Invest Development Co. Ltd
Site area: 28,831 square meters
Total floor area: 124,000 square meters
Concrete, brick
Tile, stone, glass, curtain wall
In cooperation with Fangjia Architecture Design Co. Ltd

This project is located on the north side of the Shenzhen central business district. It is surrounded by the beautiful landscape of the Xiangmi holiday resort, and opposite the main thoroughfare is a golf course. It is an ideal site for a residential project.

The architectural design exploits the peaceful environment. The dominant building structure is a 12-story apartment block, each floor comprising two units with sweeping 180 degree views. Most of the apartments are located on a north–south axis in order to utilize natural light and improve ventilation. All parking is located underground in order to preserve the available green area, to provide a greater level of community facilities, and to minimize noise and traffic congestion at ground level.

High-rise apartments are located within the 12-story apartment blocks. These high-rise apartments have their own architectural expression, but one which also stresses the continuity of the overall development. The facades, which are European in style, are finished in shades of yellow and green, integrating the buildings with their garden-like surroundings. The result is a tranquil residential district of high quality.

1

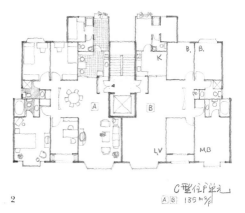

2

3

1 Type A apartment plan
2 Type C plan of 12-story apartment
3 Part of elevation
4 Aerial view

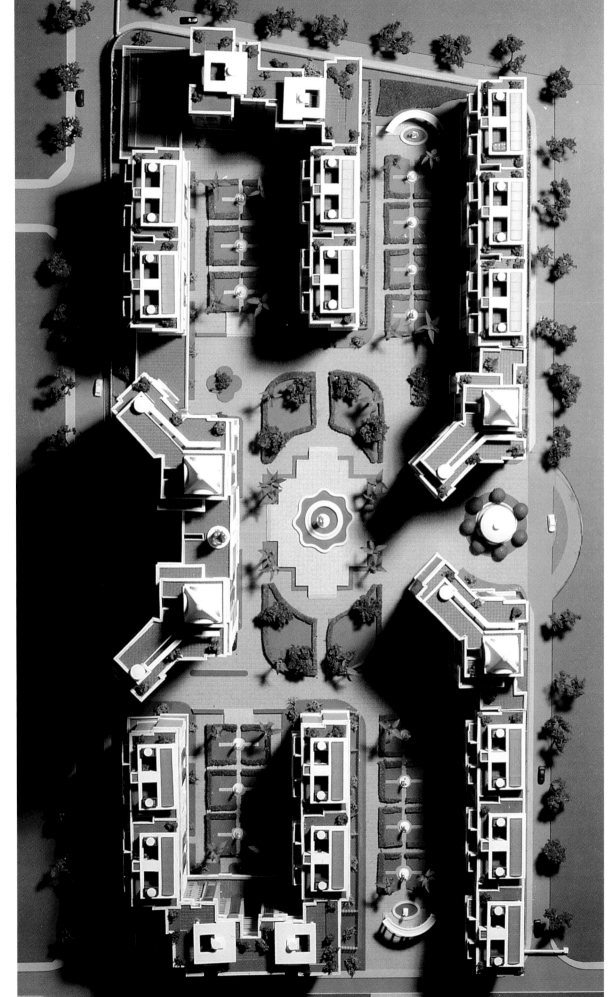

4

5 Elevation sketch
6 View from north
7 Concept sketch
8 General view from south

6

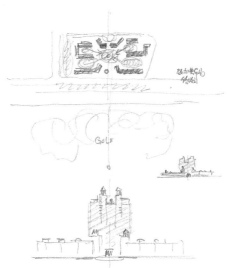

7

8

Futian Residential Development

Competition 1997
Shenzhen, China
Hutchison Whampoa Properties Ltd
Site area: 156,394 square meters
Total floor area: 469,100 square meters
Concrete
Stone, glass, tile, curtain wall
Winning international competition entry

This project is located within the new central development district of Futian, in one of the few remaining undeveloped areas in the heart of Shenzhen. In order to meet the need for a medium-density residential development, and also to preserve as much of the existing open space as possible, a unique design approach is adopted.

Based on the site layout, a series of 29-story high-rise apartment buildings are located along an ellipse placed symmetrically on the site. A huge open space, known as a district activity center, is created at the middle of the ellipse. This is used for parks, sports activities, an entertainment area, and community services including child care and a playground. The district activity center is built above ground level to allow for traffic flow underneath. A well-designed footpath provides easy access. A large terrace is also created in conjunction with the apartment towers. This provides more garden space on the terrace level and underground parking for residents. In fact, all district parking is located underground to avoid noise pollution.

Continued

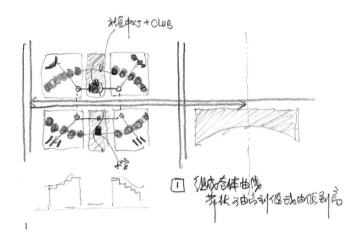

1

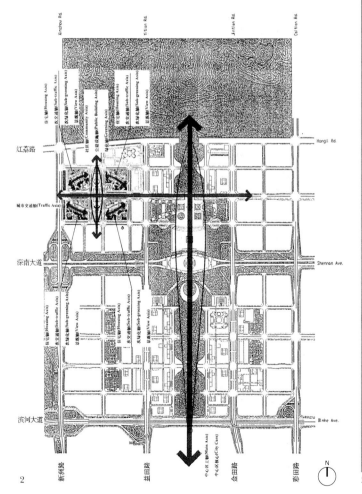

2

3

224

1 Concept sketch
2 Sketch showing location in the new central development district of Futian
3 Master plan

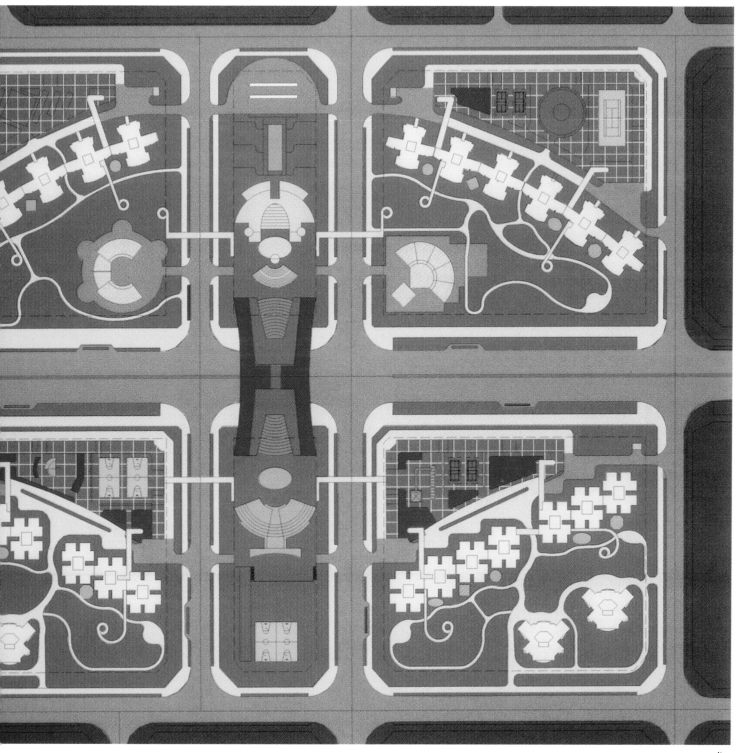

The district traffic system is well integrated with other sections of the city.

All residents can take advantage of the extensive views from both the front and rear of their apartment towers. Various unit sizes are included in the floor plan to cater for different family needs. All floor layouts and sections are designed for optimal orientation, ventilation, and natural light, and to maximize internal space.

The project master plan takes into consideration the district ecosystem, green space requirements, traffic noise and pollution, and other environmental concerns, and provides possible models for future urban residential developments in other major metropolises in China.

4 Elevation sketch
5 Aerial view of model showing the site location near city hall
6 View of model from southeast
7 General view
8 Initial study sketch of spatial relationships

4

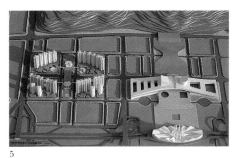

5

6

7

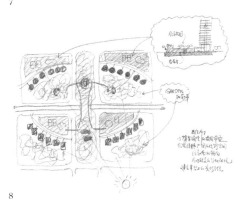

8

Mingzhu Building

Design/Completion 1996/2000
Beijing, China
Hutchison Whampoa Properties Ltd (Hong Kong)
Site area: 7,300 square meters
Total floor area: 34,000 square meters
Concrete
Stone, curtain wall, metal panel

The building is located in the eastern commercial and business district of Beijing. According to the master plan, the structure should conform in height and style with the existing high-rise hotels, office buildings, and department stores on the main streets.

The building envelope is based on a rectangular structure with the addition of curved glass curtain walls. Each floor contains 10 luxury apartments with natural lighting and ventilation. The top two floors house luxury villa units. South-facing windows are a priority in the design, and the allocation between living space and office space in all apartments is flexible.

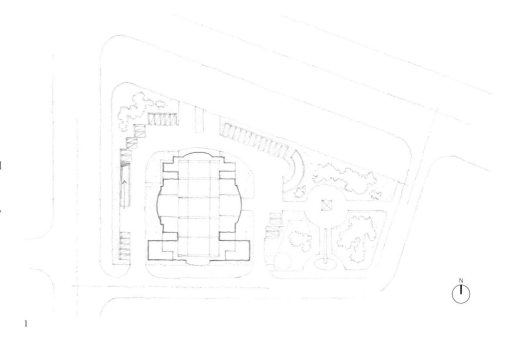

1

1   Site plan
2   Street view of model from north
3   Typical apartment level plan
4   Perspective

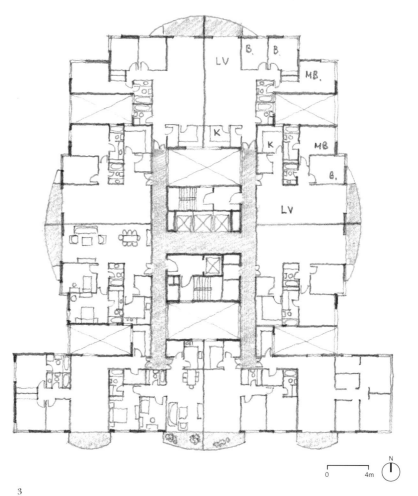

2   3

4

Fengrun Garden

Design/Completion 1992/1998
Shenzhen, China
Fengrun Investment Co. Ltd
Site area: 180,000 square meters
Total floor area: 329,684 square meters
Concrete and brick
Tile, glass, stone

Fengrun Garden is a residential project comprising mainly low- and mid-rise buildings, together with some high-rise buildings and villas. To help finance the development, the client required that the villas and multistory buildings be erected first.

All the buildings are grouped by type, and each group encloses its own courtyard and activity space. Repetition of a standard grouping produces a cohesive feeling in the project while offering variety in the orientation of individual apartments. Irregular curved footpaths connect the groups, providing accessibility while retaining the balanced spacing between groups.

1

2

3

4

5

1   Concept sketch
2   View from east
3   View from central garden
4   Elevation of mid-rise apartment building
5   Aerial view of model from southwest

Residential Building, Haifengyuan

Schematic design/Completion 1980/1994
Shenzhen, China
China Overseas Building Development Co. Ltd
Site area: 6,240 square meters
Total floor area: 62,567 square meters
Concrete
Glass, tile, paint
In cooperation with China Southwest Architectural Design & Research Institute

This project is one of the first high-rise apartment buildings designed for the city center. The first floor of the three-story podium is used for shops. The second and third floors are for office and commercial use. The seven 27-story towers contain apartments in two configurations: two bedrooms with one sitting room; and three bedrooms with two sitting rooms.

Because of the region's warm and humid climate, open corridors are used in the podium. On average, three sides of each apartment are utilized to provide natural light and ventilation, particularly to kitchens and bathrooms. These design features preserve aspects of the traditional architecture of the region.

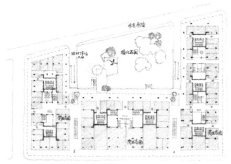

1

1   Ground level plan
2   Street view from south

2

First Meilin Village

Competition 1997
Shenzhen, China
Shenzhen Housing Bureau
Site area: 396,000 square meters
Total floor area: 833,200 square meters
Concrete
Glass, tile, paint

The site is at the edge of the beautiful Meilin Reservoir. It is a 1,500-meter-long, 50-meter-wide green space connecting two leech orchards, one to the east and the other to the west.

The site's natural garden features are stressed in the design. In this garden setting are placed public facilities, including a seniors' home, a youth club, and a children's fair; a small park with statues and a teahouse provide places for rest, recreation, and walking. The green belt becomes the primary means of communication in the project. Overpasses radiate outwards from this belt to housing clusters, forming an efficient pedestrian system with links to bus stations, shops, a middle school, a primary school, and additional recreation facilities. In this way, function and scenery are combined. Car parks are located underground and on various levels above grade.

1   Master plan sketch
2   Floor plan variations for different sized families
3   Aerial view of model showing the central green belt

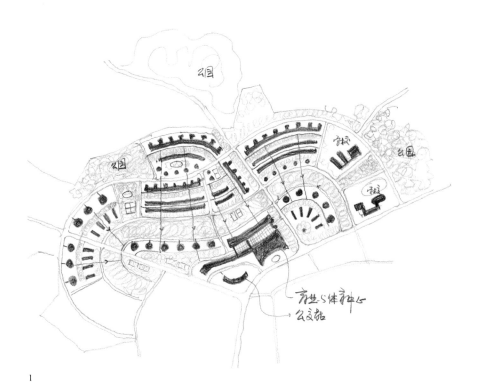

1

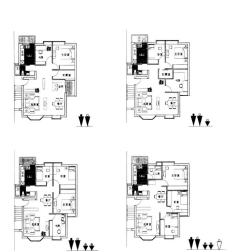

2

3

Residential Development

Competition 1997
Shenzhen, China
Henderson (China) Investment Co. Ltd
Site area: 136,000 square meters
Total floor area: 405,000 square meters
Concrete, brick
Tile, glass, paint
Winning international competition entry

The residential area of downtown Shenzhen is composed of five sections, and is located near the city's main north–south axis, the City Hall, Citizen Square, and the Lianhuashan scenic area.

The overall plan of this project uses three axes to create an organic connection with the master plan of the city. At the junction of the five residential sections there is a green space, under which are located car parks and roads. This green space provides residents with a pleasant environment, and also connects the residential apartments to department stores, schools, kindergartens, and other facilities. It also allows separation of pedestrian and vehicular traffic, creating an ideal living environment within the existing road network.

The design of the residential apartments takes into account the regional geographic characteristics and weather conditions of Shenzhen. For example, towers of a given design are associated with the apartments in a manner that accords with the Shenzhen climate. Apartment orientation is carefully planned to ensure good lighting and ventilation while avoiding the glare of the afternoon sun. Adequate spaces are provided between towers, and apartments of different sizes are available to suit individual needs.

The overall design attempts to provide a combination of quality interior and exterior environments in a new and wholesome form that will suit the coming century.

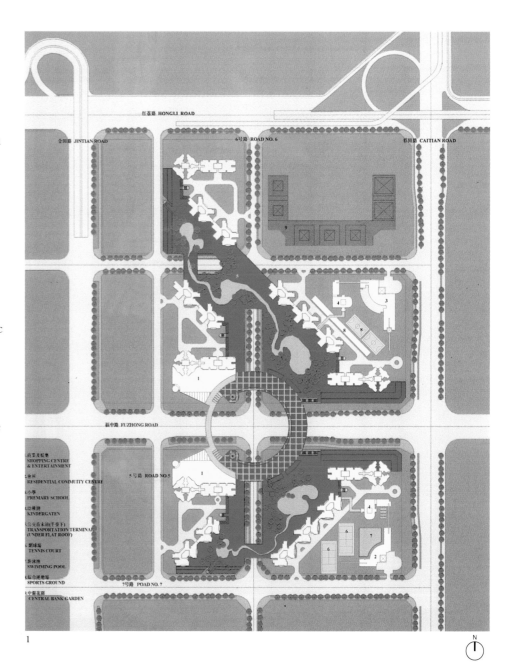

1

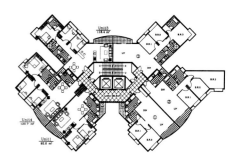

2

1   Site plan
2   Apartment plans
3   Aerial view

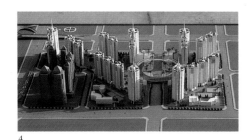

4

5

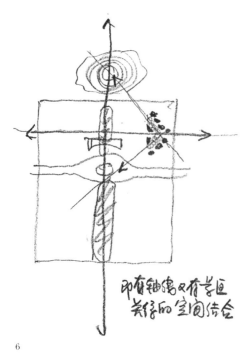

6

7

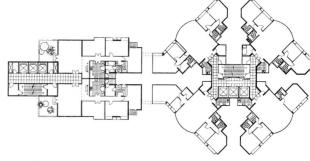

8

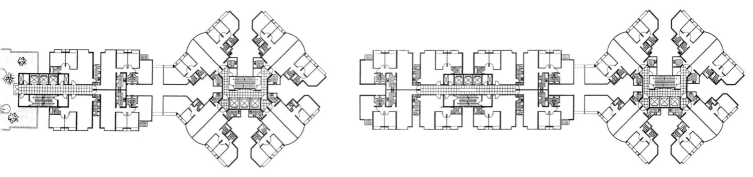

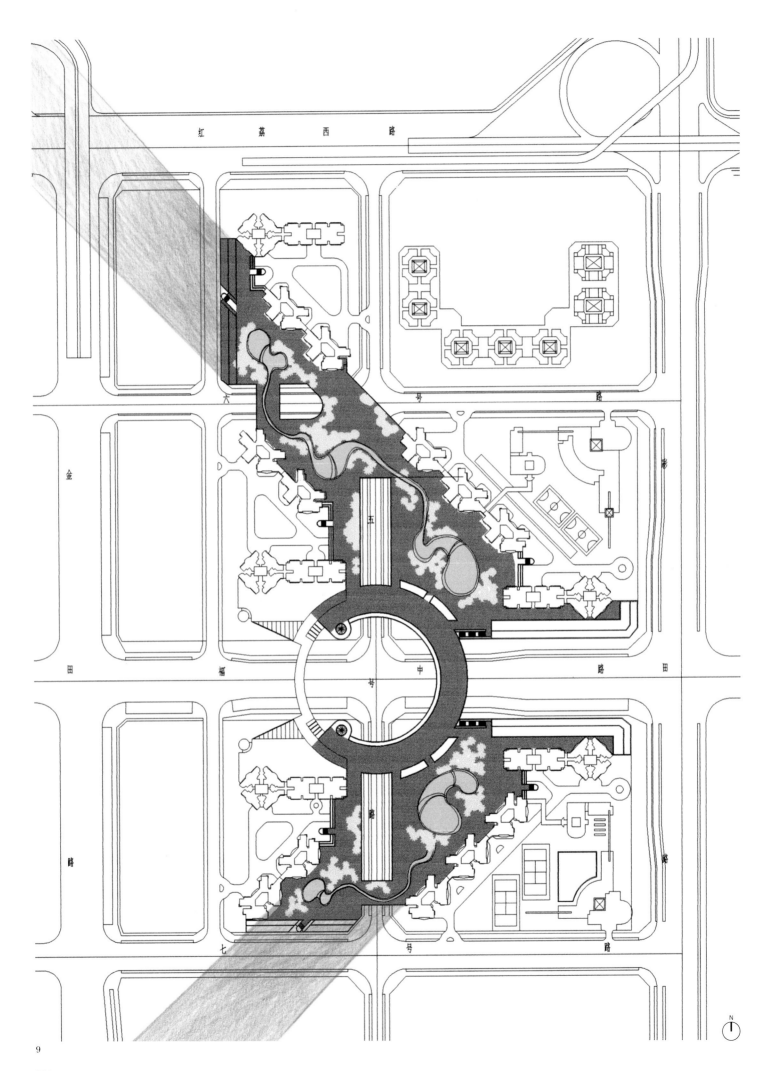

红荔西路

9 Garden terrace
10 Section detail showing the relationship between the parking and apartment spaces
11 Layout plan illustrating path of sunlight
12 Terrace view from south

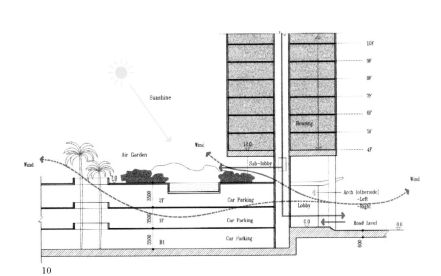

10

11

12

FIRM PROFILE

Biography

Chen Shi Min

After graduating from Chongqing Institute of Architecture and Engineering (CIAE) in 1954, I was assigned a job in Beijing with the Beijing Institute of Industrial Architectural Design (BIIAD). BIIAD was one of the top design organizations in mainland China at the time. It was sponsored and controlled by the central government. It brought together many top designers and well-known domestic architects and provided an excellent opportunity for architects to pursue various design projects on a national scale. For me, it was an enormously rich field of learning experiences.

Chinese architecture of the early 1950s was influenced both by Chinese tradition and by the modern Russian style. It answered a very basic functional and spatial need. The common features of the architectural language were a Chinese rooftop of colored glazed tiles, a basic rectangular shape, and a colonnaded entrance with symmetrical buildings attached on both sides. The management structure of the design institute was also in line with the Russian model, which combined architecture and engineering services (civil, electrical, mechanical, etc.) in an institute structure.

In 1954 China was in a strong phase of construction. New buildings were waiting to be built and old ones being refurbished. At 19, I was already involved in countless projects under the supervision of the top designers in BIIAD, ranging from industrial factories, government offices, and research centers to university colleges, embassies, and residences. After four years, which I regard as my "foundation" years in architecture, I gradually became confident in design and began to take charge of projects on my own.

From 1958 the so-called "Great Leap Forward" spread across mainland China. The initial objective of this government initiative was to speed up the rate of development in China in order to catch up with the West. Under this political climate, the building industry was pushed into the front line. Ten large public buildings were to be built in Beijing alone to celebrate the tenth anniversary of the establishment of the People's Republic. These projects included the Assembly Hall, National Opera House, National Art Gallery, National Museum, and National Cinema. Design competitions were held by the government to achieve the best outcome, and this stimulated Chinese design to new heights.

I was engaged as a design assistant for the National Opera House and National Cinema design competitions. Our scheme for a 6,318-seat opera house was accepted by Premier Zhou Enlai. Although the project did not proceed for financial reasons, it taught us how to participate in design competitions, present a proposal, and stress its key features and its advantages over other schemes. Our team subsequently won the competition for the National Cinema project.

In the following years I had the opportunity to work on many large projects as a core member of BIIAD. In 1959 I provided two design schemes for an assembly hall for 2,000 people in Qingdao city, which received the second and the third awards (no first award was given). In 1980 I won the second and third prizes in the Beijing Residential House Competition, and in 1981 I won an award in a national small-to-medium size theater design competition. Participating in these competitions helped to form my design identity, based on my interpretation of architecture.

Chen Shi Min

By the mid-1960s another political movement—the "Cultural Revolution"—was sweeping across mainland China. My family, like thousands of intellectual families, was sent away from Beijing to a remote part of the countryside in Henan province, south of the Yellow River, to work on farms. It was not until the spring of 1971 that I returned to Beijing with a few architects on a mission to design the National Guest House, on the request of Premier Zhou Enlai. Soon after, the government decided to re-establish BIIAD, and in late 1972 my family was finally transferred back to Beijing and I was able to resume my design activities.

The period between 1972 and 1980 was an important developmental stage in my career. I began to be involved in national key projects, such as the Memorial Hall of Revolutionaries on Tian An Men Square in Beijing, as well as overseas projects sponsored by the Chinese government, including the National Stadium in Pakistan and the Assembly Hall in Guinea. In May 1976 I was appointed to take control of the Beijing National Library project, the biggest library of its kind in China. It contained more than 20 million items with a total construction area of 160,000 square meters. The project involved hundreds of architects. As the project architect, I was responsible for the schematic design and liaison with the government for approval, spanning a period of five years from the initial design scheme to the final stage of the documentation. This project widened my field of vision and brought me to the front line in the design of large key projects in China.

Following the announcement of China's "Open Door" policy in the 1980s, I published several articles in the *Chinese Architectural Journal*. In these articles I stated that a design should not only follow the basic pragmatic principles of being applicable, economical, and artistic, but should also involve a search for different building envelopes, structures, and materials in response to the country's new social contexts. I believed that architecture should reflect these changes. To achieve this, we needed to study our Chinese vernacular characteristics and architectural "yardsticks" to create a new dimension, sympathetic with the local environment, climate, conditions, and landscape. In addition, this new architectural identity should draw from overseas experience and practice, to explore new ideas and directions, to create new forms, and to address new building technologies and the process of urban growth.

Early 1980 was a turning point in my life: I was appointed by BIIAD to establish Watson Architecture & Engineering Design Consultants in Hong Kong. Our objective was to expand BIIAD services into Hong Kong and the wider Asian region. Hong Kong was an amorphous commercial conurbation in the early 1980s—complex, vigorous, and completely different to Communist China. The architectural landscape was a mixture of highly prestigious commercial skyscrapers and humble, run-down, low-rise apartments. There were hundreds of architectural firms already fighting in an extremely competitive market. Architects from the mainland were used to working in the low-consumption, non-commercial society of China; it was a great challenge for us to survive in Hong Kong, one of the most capitalist territories in the world.

Although Watson was partially sponsored by BIIAD, it appeared in Hong Kong as a private company that lacked local connections, financial backing, and knowledge of the Hong Kong market. As most of us were Mandarin-speaking, we had great difficulty even understanding the local Cantonese. The company's first two projects were a group of three townhouses and a 60,000-square-meter high-rise apartment in Shenzhen, China's new economic zone adjoining Hong Kong.

In early 1983 Watson obtained its first real project, the Nanhai Hotel in Shekou, Shenzhen. The major investors in this project, the Hong Kong Shanghai Bank, Miramar Hotel & Investment, and the Bank of China, initially planned to employ overseas architects and interior designers for this five-star hotel, as they considered that no mainland Chinese architects were capable of designing a project of such high quality. They were also looking for an experienced project manager outside China to manage the hotel's construction. After various negotiations, the clients accepted my design proposal, inviting me to be the project architect. Due to the outstanding architectural design, the client commissioned me to provide the interior fitout for the hotel. In order to smooth the project construction, I was also appointed project manager, with responsibility for more than 28 sub-contractors from both Hong Kong and mainland China.

In order to have a better understanding of the client and the American way of running a project, I visited many top architectural firms in America, including Skidmore, Owings and Merrill (SOM) and the Portman company. Portmans, in particular, left me with a deep impression: I was fascinated by their design ideologies, their approaches, and their way of running an architectural practice. I was particularly impressed with the concepts and techniques used in dealing with hotel atria and the open space inside public buildings. At an early stage of the Nanhai project, I went to the Portman Hong Kong office and worked there for more than a month. This was one of my most valuable experiences: it gave me an introduction to American design, which was very different from Chinese and Russian design approaches. Even now, I still appreciate their techniques in handling atrium spaces in hotels and public buildings. In the end, the building was completed not only on time, but also below budget, and was greatly appreciated by the clients and the public.

Following the success of the Nanhai Hotel and a few other projects, Watson established itself as a recognized architectural firm in the Shenzhen region. In 1986 I was transferred from Watson to the China Real Estate Development Holding Co. (CRED) to establish Hua Yi Designing Consultants, its overseas subsidiary. As the chief architect and general manager, my tasks were to set up the new office in Hong Kong and to provide architectural services to China, Hong Kong, and overseas.

My responsibility in Hua Yi was expanded from a purely design-oriented role to the position of running a financially independent architectural practice. Within an eight-year period, Hua Yi went through various stages of change, surviving in an extremely competitive commercial climate.

It grew from an initial staff of five to an organization of more than 100 people in 1995, spread over several offices. With hundreds of influential projects in China and overseas to its credit, Hua Yi is now one of the most respected architectural firms in China.

With the opening of the Chinese market, many well-known international firms have entered the Chinese domestic scene and this has made the already competitive market even tougher. In order to evolve, Hua Yi has to be internationally competitive. I have visited many architectural firms around the world and met many famous architects including I.M. Pei, Kisho Kurokawa, and others in order to learn from them on various aspects of architecture, particularly in relation to company structure, management, and modern technologies. I have also created opportunities to work with some overseas companies on individual projects to develop a good working relationship. These include Peddle Thorp Architects (Australia), B+H Architects and Jacques Beique & Associates (Canada), and Seed Consultants Co, Ltd, Nara (Japan). Through such cooperation and exchange, Hua Yi has rapidly adopted international standard design approaches and methodologies and applied them in practice, boosting its confidence and enhancing its ability to achieve further success in the competitive new China.

In the past eight years, despite most of my time being spent on marketing and the day-to-day management of the company, I have still been deeply involved in design and in charge of major projects, from the initial concept to the final documentation. After more than 43 years of practice, my understanding of architecture has become more mature and I am in the "golden age" of my career as a designer. Since moving to Hong Kong in 1980, I have had the opportunity to pursue more than 60 projects with a total area of 5,000,000 square meters. Faced with this volume of design opportunities, I have begun to search for new design solutions in order to explore new paths in architecture.

In late 1996, Chinese officials loosened their previous policies to allow well-recognized architects to register a private architectural practice under their own name. This gave me a unique opportunity to fulfill a dream, and on 28 October 1996, after careful consideration and planning, Chen Shi Min Architects Ltd was formed. The new company will be used as a platform to extend my career in architecture in my later years, focusing mainly on:

- design research and development

- public buildings, city planning, and urban design (particularly housing design)

- best architectural practice

- training.

To date, Chen Shi Min Architects has secured many influential projects in the face of stiff international competition, and its business activities extend to many cities across China.

1

2

7

3

4

8

5

1 Chen Shi Min's home town, Ya An, in Sichuan Province
2 Childhood
3 Students at Chongqing Institute of Architecture and Engineering
4 After graduating, Chen Shi Min and his wife, Hon Lam, started working together
5 With two famous Chinese architects, Ting Bao Yang (middle) and Le Yi Lin (left) at the Great Wall, 1976
6 With his family, Beijing, 1968
7 On first arriving in Hong Kong as overseas general representative in 1980
8 Receiving the title and certificate of China Design Master, 1994
9 Meeting with leaders of the Chinese Government, 1994

6

9

Chen Shi Min

October 1935	Born in Ya An, Sichuan Province, China
1952–1954	Student, Department of Architecture, Chongqing Institute of Architecture and Engineering
1954–1966	Architect, Beijing Institute of Architecture and Engineering Design
1967–1970	Labourer, Henan Province (Cultural Revolution)
1970–1973	Architect, Henan Architectural Design Institute
1973–1980	Project Architect, China Architectural Science and Research Institute
1981–1985	Senior Architect and Vice-Chief Architect, Hong Kong Watson Architecture and Engineering Design Consultants Ltd
1986–1989	Chief Architect and Overseas General Representative, China Real Estate Development Holding Co. (CRED)
	Manager, China Sculpture and Mural (Overseas) Co.
	General Manager and Chief Architect, Hua Yi Designing Consultants Ltd (Hong Kong)
1990–present	Vice-Chairman, General Manager, and Chief Architect, Hua Yi Designing Consultants Ltd (Hong Kong)
	Executive Director, Hua Yi Designing Consultants (Tokyo) Ltd
	General Manager and Chief Architect, Hua Yi Designing Consultants Ltd (Shenzhen)
1996–present	Chairman, Chen Shi Min Architects Ltd

Professional Membership and Social Titles

1970–present	Member, China Architects Association
1980–1985	Member, China Architectural Design Committee
1983–1985	Member, Shenzhen Architectural Design Committee
1983–1985	Chief Architectural Consultant, Shenzhen Urban Planning Bureau
1986–present	Consultant, Shenzhen Urban Planning Committee
	Director, Shenzhen Architecture Society
	Vice Chairman and Consultant Architect, China Sculpture and Mural Co.
	Chief Architect, Nara China Cultural Village Co., Japan
	Chief Consultant, Japan Nara Nichinichi Newspapers Co., Japan
1996–present	Committee board member, China Architects Association

Professional Qualifications

1954	BA in Architecture, Chongqing Institute of Architecture and Engineering
1982	Senior Architect Award (national title)
1987	Professor Level Senior Architect Award (national title)
1994	National Design Master Award (national title)

10

11

12

13

14

10 Working in co-operation with architect Antony Rossi of Peddle Thorp, Australia

11 Meeting with Japanese design master, Kisho Kurokawa

12 Group meeting with architects of Hua Yi Designing Consultants

13 Meeting with famous Canadian architect, Mr. Arthur Erikson in Shenzhen, 1997

14 Working with the architects of Chen Shi Min Architects Ltd

Chronological List of Buildings & Projects

* Indicates work featured in this book
(see Selected and Current Works).

Beijing Institute of Architecture and Engineering Design

Biological Product Research Institute
Shanxi, China
1956

Capital Movie Palace
Beijing, China
Scheme
(Participant)
1958

City Planning For Zhangan Street
Beijing, China
Scheme
(Participant)
1959

National Theater
Beijing, China
(Participant)
1959

Politics & Law Building
Beijing, China
(Participant)
1959

National Conference Building
Conakry, Guinea
(Participant)
1964

China Architectural Science and Research Institute

State House
Beijing, China
(Participant)
1970/1971

National Memory Museum of Tian An Men Square
Beijing, China
(Participant)
1975

National Stadium of Pakistan
Islamabad, Pakistan
(Participant)
1978

National Library
Beijing, China
(Head of Architect Group)
1976/1980

Watson Architecture & Engineering Design Consultants Ltd

*Residential Building, Haifengyuan
Shenzhen, China
In cooperation with China Southwest Architectural Design &
Research Institute
Schematic design
1980/1994

Botanical Garden Club of Guangzhou
Guangzhou, China
Scheme
1981

Unification Residential District
Shenzhen, China
Scheme
1982

*Nanhai Hotel
Shekou, China
Associate architect: Watson Architecture & Engineering Design
Consultants Ltd
1983/1985

*Shenzhen Financial Center
Shenzhen, China
In cooperation with Shenzhen Project & Research Institute of
NMIC (China)
Schematic & preliminary design
1983/1986

International Conference of Sivil Lank
Shenzhen, China
Scheme
1985/1987

Hua Yi Designing Consultants Ltd

Interior for Construction Bank
Shenzhen, China
1986/1987

Interior for Business & Industry Bank
Shenzhen, China
1986/1987

*Chinese Cultural Village
Nara, Japan
In cooperation with Seed Consultants Co. Ltd, Nara (Japan)
1986 (under construction)

*Qin Xing Hotel
Xian, China
In cooperation with China Northwest Building Design & Research
Institute
1986

*Shatian Baofu Cemetery
Hong Kong, China
Joint venture with Chung Hua Nan Architects Ltd Hong Kong
1986/1989

*International Commercial and Residential Building
Shenzhen, China
1986/1988

Painting Master House
Beijing, China
1987/1989

Automatic Equipment Office
Beijing, China
1988

Tian Fu Restaurant
Nara, Japan
1988

Nine Dragon Restaurant
Tokyo, Japan
Scheme
1988

*Hua Du Garden
Shenzhen, China
1988/1993

Tai Lank Resort Village
Wuxi, China
Scheme
1988

*Hotel Sinomonde
Montreal, Canada
In cooperation with Jacques Beique Architect, Montreal (Canada)
1988/1991

*Tianan International Building
Shenzhen, China
In cooperation with China Electronics Eng. Design Institute
Winning international competition entry
1988/1993

*Foreign Trade Center Building
Shenzhen, China
Schematic & preliminary design
1988/1996

*Shenzhen Railway Station
Shenzhen, China
Joint venture with Shenzhen Project & Research Institute of NMIC
1989/1992

French Paris Floating Restaurant
Paris, France
Scheme
1990

*International Trade Plaza
Shenzhen, China
1990/1996

*Huamin Plaza
Shenzhen, China
1991/1995

Laon Kai Hotel
Laon Kai, Thailand
Scheme
1991

Macau Commercial Building
Macau
Scheme
1991

*Imperial Capital Hotel
Louyang, China
Scheme
1991

*International Science and Technology Building
Shenzhen, China
In cooperation with Mechanical Electron Industry Ministry and
Engineering Design Research Institute, Shenzhen Branch (China)
1991/1996

*Office Building, Gintian
Shenzhen, China
1991/1994

*The Flying Saucer Nightclub
Shenzhen, China
Winning competition entry
1988/1991

Art Museum of Yaun Ma Bu
Tokyo, Japan
Scheme
1992

*Shum Yip Building
Haerbin, China
In cooperation with Architecture Design Institute of Heilongjing
(China)
1992/1995

*Foreign Trade Center
Shenzhen, China
In cooperation with Peddle Thorp Architects (Australia)
Competition
1992

*Fengrun Garden
Shenzhen, China
1992/1998

*Huafu Center
Fuzhou, China
Winning competition entry
1992

*Hualu Chuanglu International Building
Jinan, China
Competition
1992

*Mingru Hotel
Beihai, China
Schematic & preliminary design
1992

*Baofa Building
Shenzhen, China
Preliminary design
1992

*Development Bank Building, Shenzhen
Shenzhen, China
Schematic design in cooperation with Peddle Thorp Architects
(Australia)
Winning competition entry
1992/1996

Macau Haojing Hotel
Macau
(Interior design)
1993/1995

*Commercial and Apartment Building, Caiwuwei
Shenzhen, China
1993/1999

*Well Bond Grand Hotel
Shenzhen, China
Scheme
1993

*Chief Fine Building
Nanjing, China
1994/1999

*Great World Commercial Center
Dalian, China
In cooperation with Peddle Thorp Architects (Australia),
Dalian Architectural Design & Research Institute
Winning international competition entry
Schematic & preliminary design
1994/1999

*International Hotel and Commercial Plaza
Guangzhou, China
Winning international competition entry
Schematic design
1994–1995

*Hongji Commercial Center
Tianjin, China
In cooperation with Tianjin Municipal Engineering Design &
Research Institute (China)
Winning international competition entry
Schematic & preliminary design
1994/1999

Shenzhen Newspaper Complex Building
Shenzhen, China
Competition
1994

*Wango Plaza
Guangzhou, China
Schematic & preliminary design
Winning international competition entry
1994–1995

*Shanglong Building
Shenzhen, China
Winning international competition entry
1994/1999

*Qilin Resort
Shenzhen, China
1995/1997

*Seg Plaza
Shenzhen, China
Winning competition entry
1995/1999

*Commercial Town, Futian
Shenzhen, China
Winning competition entry
1995/1999

*Fenglong Center
Shenzhen, China
Competition
1995

*Architecture Cultural Center, Beijing
Beijing, China
Winning international competition entry
1995/1999

*China Construction Corporation Complex, Chongqing
Chongqing, China
In cooperation with Chongqing Iron & Steel Designing Institute
1996/1999

*Agricultural Bank, Shandong
Jinan, China
In cooperation with Zhongian Architectural Design Institute
of Jinan (China)
Winning competition entry
Schematic & preliminary design
1996/1999

*Bocom Finance Tower
Shanghai, China
Competition
1996

*Communication Bank Building, Suzhou Branch
Suzhou, China
Competition
1996

*Shenzhen City Hall
Shenzhen, China
Scheme
1996

*State Guest House
Shenzhen, China
Competition
1996

*Huanqing Building
Shenzhen, China
Competition
1997

*Daxin Building
Chongqing, China
In cooperation with China Southwest Architectural Design
& Research Institute
1997/2000

Jiang Su TV Station
Najing, China
Winning competition entry
1997

Chen Shi Min Architects Ltd

*New Downtown Shenzhen
Shenzhen, China
Runner-up, international competition
1996

*Mingzhu Building
Beijing, China
1996/2000

*Qiaoguang Plaza
Shenzhen, China
Joint venture with China Aeronautical Project & Design Institute
Schematic design
1997

*Pingan Plaza
Shanghai, China
In cooperation with East China Architectural Design & Research
Institute
Schematic & preliminary design
1997/2000

*First Meilin Village
Shenzhen, China
Competition
1997

*International Conference and Exhibition Center
Qingdao, China
Competition
1997

*Shopping Mall in New Downtown
Shenzhen, China
Joint venture with Peddle Thorp Architects (Australia)
Winning international competition entry
1997

*Futian Residential Development
Shenzhen, China
Winning international competition entry
1997

*Rose Garden
Shenzhen, China
In cooperation with Fangjia Architecture Design Co. Ltd
Schematic design
1997/2000

*Residential Development
Shenzhen, China
Winning international competition entry
1997

City Administration Center
Lianyungang, China
1997/2000

Villa of Sand River Golf Club
Shenzen, China
1998/1999

Selected Awards & Competitions

Awards

Beijing Excellent Design Award
Capital City Planning & Construction Committee, Beijing
Architecture Cultural Center, Beijing
Beijing, China
1997

Third Prize, Excellent Design Awards
China State Construction Engineering Co.
Great World Commercial Center
Dalian, China
1996

Third Prize, Excellent Design Awards
China State Construction Engineering Co.
International Science and Technology Building
Shenzhen, China
1996

Second Prize, Excellent Design Awards
China State Construction Engineering Co.
Commercial Town, Futian
Shenzhen, China
1996

Second Prize, Excellent Design Awards
China State Construction Engineering Co.
Shanglong Building
Shenzhen, China
1996

First Prize, Excellent Design Awards
China State Construction Engineering Co.
Seg Plaza
Shenzhen, China
1996

Second Prize, Excellent Design Awards
China State Construction Engineering Co.
Office Building, Gintian
Shenzhen, China
1996

First Prize, Excellent Design Awards
China State Construction Engineering Co.
Hongji Commercial Center
Tianjin, China
1996

Third Prize, Shenzhen Excellent Design Awards
Shenzhen Construction Bureau
Office Building, Gintian
Shenzhen, China
1995

Second Prize, Shenzhen Excellent Design Awards
Shenzhen Construction Bureau
Tianan International Building
Shenzhen, China
1994

Second Prize, Shenzhen Excellent Design Awards
Shenzhen Construction Bureau
Hua Du Garden
Shenzhen, China
1994

Second "Architect Cup" Excellent Design Award
National Middle-Aged and Young Architect Works Competition
Hongji Commercial Center
Tianjin, China
1994

Second Prize, Excellent Design Awards
China State Construction Engineering Co.
Shenzhen Railway Station
Shenzhen, China
1993

First Prize, Shenzhen Excellent Design Awards
Shenzhen Construction Bureau
Shenzhen Railway Station
Shenzhen, China
1993

Excellent Design Prize
China Architecture Association
Nanhai Hotel
Shekou, China
1993

First Prize, Excellent Design Awards
China State Construction Engineering Co.
Hotel Sinomonde
Montreal, Canada
1992

Prestigious Award
Holiday Inn Worldwide
Hotel Sinomonde
Montreal, Canada
1992

Excellent Design Award
Guangdong Province
Shenzhen Financial Center
Shenzhen, China
1988

Third Prize, National Excellent Design Awards
Nanhai Hotel
Shekou, China
1986

Competitions

Winner
Residential Development
Shenzhen, China
International open tender
1997

Winner
Shopping Mall in New Downtown
Shenzhen, China
International open tender
1997

Runner-up
New Downtown Shenzhen
Shenzhen, China
International invited competition
1996

Winner
Architecture Cultural Center, Beijing
Beijing, China
International open tender
1995

Winner
Commercial Town, Futain
Shenzhen, China
Open tender
1995

Winner
Seg Plaza
Shenzhen, China
Open tender
1995

Winner
Shanglong Building
Shenzhen, China
International open tender
1994

Winner
Wango Plaza
Guangzhou, China
International invited competition
1994

Winner
Hongji Commercial Center
Tianjin, China
International open tender
1994

Winner
Great World Commercial Center
Dalian, China
International open tender
1994

Winner
Huafu Center
Fuzhou, China
International open tender
1992

Winner
Foreign Trade Center Building
Shenzhen, China
International open tender
1992

Winner
International Science and Technology Building
Shenzhen, China
Open tender
1991

Winner
The Flying Saucer Nightclub
Shenzhen, China
Invited competition
1988

Winner
Tianan International Building
Shenzhen, China
International invited competition
1988

Second and Third Prize
National competition
Beijing Residential House
Beijing, China
1980

Second Prize
(No First Prize awarded)
Qindao Great Hall of People's Conference
Qindao, China
1959

Winner
Jiang Su TV Station
Nanjing, China
Open tender
1997

Selected Bibliography

"Architectural Design and Design Sketch." *Expression of Architecture* (September 1994), pp. 3–21.

"Architectural Development of Hong Kong Hotel." *Hong Kong Architecture* (1988).

"Architectural Rhythm." *China Architecture & Urbanism* (June 1991), pp. 72–80.

"Architecture Creation in the Process of Exploration." *China Architecture & Urbanism* (no. 1, 1989), pp. 98–119.

"Design Resolution: The Unavoidable Path." *Chinese Architectural Journal* (October 1994).

"Environment • People • Architectural Space: World Architecture Review." *China Architecture & Urbanism* (1988).

ERA • SPACE: Architectural Design Master Book. China Architecture & Building Press, 1995.

"Further Discussion on Modernisation of Foreign Investment and Vernacular Architectural Style." *Asian Construction* (July 1981).

"Nanhai Hotel." *Shenzhen Architectural* (April 1988).

"Introduction to Chinese Tradition and Architecture Culture." *China Architecture & Urbanism* (December 1991), pp. 56–59.

"Issues in Public Building Design." *Chinese Architectural Journal* (no. 1, 1979).

"National Identity and Architectural Style." *Chinese Architectural Journal* (no. 2, 1980).

"Persistent Searching and Success." *Chinese Architectural Journal* (no. 10, 1993).

Acknowledgments

Firstly, I would like to offer my gratitude to Mr Paul Latham and Ms Alessina Brooks of The Images Publishing Group for their generous patience, their excellent editorial work, and for inviting me to be the first Chinese architect to be included in The Master Architect Series.

Secondly, I would like to express my thanks to the boards of Hua Yi Designing Consultants and Onyi Development Ltd for their great financial support toward this book publication.

Thirdly, I would like to thank all my colleagues and staff in Hua Yi Designing Consultants and Chen Shi Min Architects companies for their great professional contributions towards this book and also for making some of the projects described in it a reality. Their names include Wang Xing Fang, Sheng Ye, Lu Qiang, Pan Yu Quan, Kong Li Xing, Liu Dar Yuan, Liang Zeng Tian, Chen Qing Quan, Lou Qing, Hon Lam, Cai Ming, Sun Jian, Wu Guo Lin, Huang Chang Zheng, Liu Jun, Wang Xing Fa, Lie Shi Jie, Liu Shi Jing, Yang Jie, Qu Quan Yin, Liu Yun Fang and Wang Jian Fen of Hua Yi Designing Consultants. Lin Ming, Zhao Guo Xing, Chen Ting of Chen Shi Min Architects Ltd etc.

Fourthly, particular thanks should be made to Mr Zhang Zhen Guang and Mr Wang for their visual materials and photographs, Ms Lu Wen Yu and Mr Lu Xing for their important assistance in bringing order to a wide range of projects and word processing work, Mr Yue Yong and others, for their initial partial project information translations. Many thanks should be made to Mr Liang Chen and Enrico Redegalli for their English translations and editing.

Finally, I would like to thank my wife, Ms Hon Lam, and my daughter, Chen Ting, and my son Chen Liang for their great inspirations, tireless support and encouragement, and all the publication related liaisons in making this book a reality.

Index